What people are saying

"Having read The Wisconsin Road Guide *... with* The Minnesota Guide to Haunted L... *...em extraordinarily interesting. I highly recommend reading this book. I found it to be factual and quite impressive. I wish them continued success in their efforts to promote credible ghost research."*

Peter James, psychic, host of the television series *Ghost Encounters,* and author of *Heaven Can You Hear Me?*

****

"Packed with the in-depth results of Lewis and Fisk's research into an absolute plethora of ghostly activity, haunted houses and eerie stories, this is an essential and highly entertaining book for anyone and everyone interested in all things spooky. For full effect, I recommend that you read their latest mighty tome by candlelight on a dark and stormy night. You will not be disappointed. Just remember to keep a careful watch over your shoulder. As our fearless authors reveal time and again, you never know what might be lurking in the shadows..."

Nick Redfern, author of *On the Trail of the Saucer Spies; Three Men Seeking Monsters*; and *Body Snatchers in the Desert*

****

"Ghost hunters? A dime a dozen, all chasing the same antiquated phantoms. Not Lewis and Fisk. They're the real deal. How this duo scares up so many fresh cases is a major mystery. Heck, when I'm dead, they'll probably find my ghost."

Richard D. Hendricks, news editor, *The Anomalist*

****

"Lewis and Fisk understand what paranormal buffs really want: details and directions. There's enough strong material here to keep the average ghosthunter on the road for months, or years. At last, a ghosthunting guide that encourages the reader to get up and go--with directions! Lewis and Fisk understand that ghost stories are best experienced in person."

Jerome Pohlen, author of *Oddball Minnesota* and the *Oddball* series of books

THE MINNESOTA ROAD GUIDE TO HAUNTED LOCATIONS

THE MINNESOTA ROAD GUIDE TO HAUNTED LOCATIONS

By Chad Lewis & Terry Fisk

Research Publishing Company
A Division of Unexplained Research, LLC

© 2005 Chad Lewis and Terry Fisk

All rights reserved. No part of this publication may be reproduced or transmitted in any form or by any means, electrical or mechanical, including photocopy, recording, or any information storage or retrieval system, without the permission in writing from the publisher.

Library of Congress Control Number: 2005908456
ISBN-13: 978-0-9762099-2-8

Printed in the United States by Documation

Unexplained Research Publishing Company
A Division of Unexplained Research, LLC
P.O. Box 2173, Eau Claire, WI 54702-2173
Email: info@unexplainedresearch.com
www.unexplainedresearch.com

Cover Design: Terry Fisk
Back Cover Photo: Rob Mattison

DEDICATION

I dedicate this book to Nisa Giaquinto for providing the greatest adventure of all!

—Chad

I dedicate this book to my beloved children and grandchildren: Stephanie, Ryan, and Robert; Chuck, Jeanne, Alyssa, Madison, and Anthony; Niles, Amber, Hailey, Drake, and Colton.

—Terry

TABLE OF CONTENTS

Preface..i
Foreword...iii
Acknowledgments..v
Introductions...vii

1 - Northeastern Minnesota   1

Aitkin (Aitkin Co.)
    40 Club Inn... 2

Buhl (St. Louis Co.)
    Lakeview Cemetery...6

Coleraine (Itasca Co.)
    Bertha's Grave... 9

Duluth (St. Louis Co.)
    Charlie's Club... 14
    Glensheen...20

Embarrass (St. Louis Co.)
    Heritage House...25

Hoyt Lakes (St. Louis Co.)
    Hoyt Lakes Memorial Cemetery.........................28

Moose Lake (Carlton Co.)
    Haunted Train Trestles...................................... 30

Stillwater (Washington Co.)
    Warden's House... 35
    Water Street Inn.. 41

Taylors Falls (Chisago Co.)
    Old Jail Bed & Breakfast....................................45

Two Harbors (Lake Co.)
    Black Woods Restaurant.. 49

2 - Northwestern Minnesota   53

Alexandria (Douglas Co.)
    Old Broadway... 54

Annandale (Wright Co.)
    Thayer's Historic Bed n' Breakfast.. 60

Anoka (Anoka Co.)
    Billy's Bar and Grill... 65
    Cal's Corner Restaurant... 70
    Durkin's Irish Pub... 73

Buffalo (Wright Co.)
    Sturges Park... 77

New York Mills (Otter Tail Co.)
    New York Mills Regional Cultural Center.................................... 82
    Whistle Stop Inn... 86

Puposky (Beltrami Co.)
    Lake Julia Sanitarium 90

Redby (Beltrami Co.)
    Redby Store.. 95

Ross (Roseau Co.)
    Wendigo.. 98

Saint Cloud (Stearns Co.)
    Skatin' Place...102

Sauk Centre (Stearns Co.)
    Oakland Cemetery..106
    The Palmer House Hotel..109

Thief River Falls (Pennington Co.)
    Dead Man's Trail 117

3 - Southeastern Minnesota   121

Dennison (Goodhue Co.)
    Vang Lutheran Church 122

Hastings (Dakota Co.)
    LeDuc Mansion 126

Mantorville (Dodge Co.)
    Phantom of the Opera House 132

Rochester (Olmsted Co.)
    Kahler Hotel 138

Wabasha (Wabasha Co.)
    Anderson House 141

Winona (Winona Co.)
    Pieces of the Past 149
    Winona Family YMCA 153

4 - Southwestern Minnesota   157

Albert Lea (Freeborn Co.)
    The Ghost of the Clock Tower 158

Elysian (Le Sueur Co.)
    Le Sueur County Historical Society Museum 162

Janesville (Waseca Co.)
    Doll House 172

Lamberton (Redwood Co.)
    Sanborn Cemetery 176

Le Sueur (Le Sueur Co.)
    Old Brewery Hill Spook Light... 179

Montgomery (Le Sueur Co.)
    Montgomery Golf Course.. 183

Pipestone (Pipestone Co.)
    Pipestone Museum... 188

5 - Twin Cities **Minnesota**   191

Brooklyn Center (Hennepin Co.)
    Regal Cinemas... 192
    Schmitt Music Centers.. 195

Maplewood (Ramsey Co.)
    Maplewood Community Center.. 199

Minneapolis (Hennepin Co.)
    Old Guthrie Theater.. 202
    Washington Street Bridge... 206

Saint Paul (Ramsey Co.)
    Fitzgerald Theatre... 211
    Forepaugh's Restaurant... 217
    Gibbs Museum.. 222
    Landmark Center... 228
    Minnesota State Fair... 233
    Wabasha Street Caves... 237

White Bear Lake (Ramsey Co.)
    Lakeshore Players Theatre.. 243

6 - Western **Minnesota**   247

Chanhassen (Carver Co.)
    Chanhassen Dinner Theatres... 248

Kimball (Stearns Co.)
　　Soap Box Laundromat 255

Montevideo (Chippewa Co.)
　　Swensson Farm Museum 258

About the Authors 263
Order Books 264

PREFACE

Corrections. Although we have made every effort to be certain that this road guide is reliable and accurate, things inevitably change and errors are made. We appreciate it if readers contact us so we can revise future editions of the book.

Updates. If you have a paranormal experience at one of these locations, please report it to us. We recommend that you keep a journal, carefully recording dates, times, locations, and what happened.

Additions. Due to lack of space, many locations had to be left out of the book. We do intend to publish a second volume. Please write and let us know of any Minnesota locations that you feel should have been included in this travel guide.

Warning. Be respectful of both the living and the dead. Several communities have had problems with people who go to these locations only to party and cause mischief. Cemeteries have been desecrated; private property has been vandalized; grounds have been littered; and buildings have been broken into.

If you do decide to check out any of the locations for yourself, please make sure that you have permission if it is private property and obey all applicable laws. Under most ordinances, cemeteries are only open from sunrise to sunset.

We will not be held responsible for any persons who decide to conduct their own investigations or for those who choose to break laws.

Disclaimer. The places listed in the book have neither been proved nor disproved to be haunted. Their inclusion in the book is based on the anecdotal reports we have received from numerous individuals. This book is for reference purposes only.

FOREWORD

Looking for Ghosts? Minnesota has them. Everywhere. Plan your next road trip for Minnesota's haunted places. It's not necessary to travel far for spine-tingling adventures. Remember . . . a sleepless night will be your reward after visiting the places Chad Lewis and Terry Fisk tell you about.

There is no need to travel around the world for some of the best haunted sites. They're found in our own backyard. Hair-raising adventures are as close as a few minutes or hours from your own home. Heck, they could be as close as your own neighborhood! Maybe you even live in a haunted area. Do you dare find out?

Minnesota is the land of 10,000 lakes—and 10,000 ghosts! It is populated by down-to-earth, hard-working people not prone to fantasy or flights of the imagination. Long winter months spent indoors are conducive to witnessing ghosts and hauntings.

We Minnesotans love the outdoors—and love ghost stories around a campfire. We are very connected to the land and have a great sense of place and history. Houses and land, farms and homes, often stay in the same family for years, passed down from generation to generation. In greater Minnesota, there's an emphasis on history and on posterity. Family-owned properties tend to stay in families, public/civic buildings, churches, schools tend to be restored and cared for—respected—not torn down and built anew, but preserved because of their historical significance in communities. Folks who are born here, often live and die here. After death they are more prone to "hang around" because of the attachment they have to the land and tradition. You betcha there are lots of ghosts in these old buildings! Minnesota has lakes, rivers, streams, dense forests, wide prairies, farm towns, port towns, big busy cosmopolitan cities, laid back main streets, roaring highways, spring, summer, fall, winter, brutal cold and snow, stifling heat and humidity, many contrasts, lots of variety, loads of things to see and experience all in one state. Old mining towns, farms, sawmills, old river towns, just the kind of places where one would expect hauntings.

At Fate, we read so many articles on haunted places/people. I admit we overlook what is in our own backyard. So, thanks to Chad and Terry for providing us with local haunts. We now have a wonderful resource to refresh ourselves with, and a renewed knowledge and love of local ghost stories.

This travel guide is conveniently arranged into sections of Minnesota so you can plan your trip to see as many haunted locations as you want. From the haunted Guthrie Theater in metropolitan Minneapolis to the spooked train trestles in Moose Lake, the North Star State is a treasure trove for ghost hunters.

This book belongs on every shelf. Whether you're a serious ghost hunter or are just mildly curious about the world of the unseen, *The Minnesota Road Guide to Haunted Locations* will be your premier travel guide from now on. Happy hauntings!

—Phyllis Galde
Editor-in-chief, Fate magazine

ACKNOWLEDGMENTS

We would like to thank Chris Belisle, Nisa Giaquinto, Richard Hendricks, Sarah Szymanski, Sharon Harvey, and Jeannine Fisk for assisting us with the research and production of this book.

We also want to thank the many people who provided us with cases, directions, and personal accounts.

INTRODUCTIONS

> I am not an adventurer by choice but by fate.
> —Vincent van Gogh

After researching vampires in Transylvania, chasing the Chupacabras in Puerto Rico, searching for the elusive monster at Loch Ness, and tracking ghosts in Ireland's castles, I have found that some of the strangest cases were right in the backyard of my neighboring state of Minnesota. In fact, we found so many ghosts in Minnesota, that I have dubbed it the land of 10,000 ghosts.

However, when people think of Minnesota they usually think of the Vikings, the Mall of America, famous gangsters, cold winters, or the beautiful lakes. Ghosts may not be the first thing that jumps into their mind. Yet when you ask people about the topic of ghosts, nearly everyone has an eerie story to tell.

What is it about ghosts and spirits that fascinate us so much? I believe that like all unexplained mysteries, humans desire to know the answers. What happens when we die? Can we "live" after death? Where do our souls go? Do we even have souls? All of these questions have plagued humans since the beginning of time. However, many skeptics blame the belief in the paranormal on media influence. With the popularity of television shows such as the *X-files*, and *Unsolved Mysteries*, along with movies like The Sixth Sense and Independence Day, it seems that paranormal phe-

INTRODUCTIONS

nomena are the new fad. Skeptics believe that the media allows people to accept unsubstantiated paranormal claims by promoting excessive attention to reports of paranormal experiences. The skeptics also claim that the media turns a critical eye when it comes to verifying the validity of paranormal claims.

Yet, belief in the paranormal, and more specifically, ghosts, has been around for much longer than scary movies. Numerous cultures and peoples throughout time have shared the belief that the human soul continues on after the death of the body. While oral stories of ghosts have been around since the beginning of human kind, one of the first written ghost stories occurred in 1450 B.C.E., where a tablet at Giza tells of a young Prince Thutme's encounter with a ghost. The prince encountered a ghost who requested that he clear sand from the rest of the previously unknown sphinx. Spooky stories that were once only told around family fires or on long carriage rides are now commonplace in the media.

Many books delve into great detail about the history of ghosts, speculating on the various theories of ghosts and haunted places. For this introduction, I have intentionally skipped the basic ghost history, as I feel this book is just as much about adventure as it is about ghosts. For me, both paranormal research and adventure go hand in hand; the two are inseparable.

The Kaiser Family Foundation states that the average adolescent spends 22 to 28 hours a week watching television. As adults, we watch even more TV—by the time we are 70, we will have spent 7 to 10 years of our lives watching TV. Why waste precious time simply watching someone have an adventure on television, when so much adventure exists in our own backyard? While it may be fun to vicariously venture into a haunted cemetery through a TV show, it is a completely different matter when you are actually there. You cannot simply change the channel when you spot shadowy figures lurking from gravestone to gravestone, and the mute button will not aid you when the ghostly wails of a mother eternally searching for her lost child haunt your eardrums.

I know, I know, there is a lot of work that goes into finding a ghost

INTRODUCTIONS

or haunted location. Most ghost stories of haunted places are filled with inaccuracies, laced with folk lore, urban legend, and extremely vague details. All of these factors make it extremely difficult to discover the truth about any given case. Throw in the lack of credible directions, and an investigation quickly becomes a real nightmare. However, do not panic. This is why we compiled the road guide. We have scoured the entire state looking for the scariest and strangest ghost cases for this guide. We have done all of the tiring legwork. We spent hours digging up the real history, we tracked down different versions of the urban legends, and we located the eyewitnesses. Now that you have the locations, the background, and even the correct directions, there is literally nothing holding you back from discovering these places.

Oh wait—what about all of the hi tech ghost hunting equipment that paranormal investigators use on TV? Although they have spent thousands of dollars on night vision, electromagnetic field meters, infrared thermometers, and motion detectors, there is no piece of equipment that will replace curiosity and common sense. Never allow the lack of equipment to impede your adventure. The best two pieces of paranormal equipment are a camera and the book you are holding in your hands.

Yet this book is only the beginning; the adventure is now firmly in your hands. Literally. Take this guide with you as you witness ghosts roaming cemeteries, pick up vanishing hitchhikers, see phantom animals, or stay overnight in a haunted hotel. The possibilities are endless, and so are the experiences that you are bound to have on your journey. You will see parts of the state that you have never seen, you may meet some odd people, see many odd things, but most of all, you will have an adventure. No one on their deathbed wished that their life had been less exciting. Now take this guide, grab a friend, and set out on your paranormal journey.

Good Luck,

Chad Lewis

INTRODUCTIONS

> Fate is the same for the man who holds back, the same if he fights hard. We are all held in a single honor, the brave with the weaklings. A man dies still if he has done nothing, as the one who has done much.
> —Homer Iliad

I was a strange child.

I grew up in a rural part of western Wisconsin and when I was about three years old, my parents purchased a rustic old farm house that was built in the 1800s. Adults might have referred to it as "rustic," but to children it was perceived as "creepy." I lived there from age three to age nine with Cindy, Ricky, and Randy—my three younger siblings. The four of us slept upstairs, and at night we sometimes felt isolated and forsaken by our parents who slept all the way downstairs. We wondered, would they even hear us if we screamed out in the middle of the night?

Another distressing factor was this mysterious door near the head of my bed. The door was consistently kept closed and off limits to us kids. The door was unique and different from all the other doors in the house, because, unlike the other doors that had doorknobs, this one was barred shut with a latch. The only other times we ever saw a door with a latch were in the illustrations from our fairy tale books. Case in point, the wicked witch had latches on the doors of her cottage in the Hansel and Gretel story. We also noticed that the giant in Jack and the Bean Stalk had latches on his door. So we knew that only evil and terrifying things resided behind doors closed with latches.

On more than one occasion, our parents had sternly warned us that we were to never open the mysterious door, and they even blocked

INTRODUCTIONS

our access to whatever was on the other side by pushing a huge dresser up against the door. But we were never quite certain if they were trying to keep us from getting in or trying to keep something from getting out. Regardless, we were convinced that whatever was behind that door could not be good.

Since we couldn't open the door, and presumably nothing could get out, we peacefully coexisted with it, and, for the most part, simply pushed it out of our minds. After a while, it seemed that there was nothing to fear in the old house, and we started to feel comfortable with playing and sleeping upstairs. But that security didn't last for long.

One night, I was reading a book to my little sister Cindy when she suddenly let out an ear-piercing scream. This scream was comparable to Drew Barrymore's scream in *ET,* or, even better, Dakota Fanning's scream in *War of the Worlds*. I had no clue as to what terrified Cindy, but that didn't stop me from cowering under the covers as she did and screaming for Mom and Dad. As it turned out, our parents could indeed hear us scream out in the middle of the night, and, without hesitation, they came running to see what was wrong. They calmed my sister down, and between sobs she described having seen a black, shadowy hand rise up from behind her bed. My parents searched behind her bed and under her bed, but found nothing. They assumed she had a nightmare, but she was awake the entire time. Maybe she imagined it? But to this day, she still remembers the event vividly and insists that it was not her imagination.

This was my first exposure to something strange and unexplained, and it left an indelible impression on my young mind. I was intrigued and wanted to know more about these bizarre creatures that lurk under our beds at night or behind closed, mysterious doors. Shortly after the black hand incident, I enlisted the help of my siblings, and together we moved the dresser that blocked the mysterious door. We lifted the latch and opened the creaking door that had not been opened in years. What we found was a huge, unfinished room that was being used as an attic for storage. The monsters that we had imagined were nowhere to be found. I was

INTRODUCTIONS

disappointed that I didn't find anything lurking there, but at the same time I felt fulfilled in knowing that I took the initiative to search for the truth by investigating the unknown.

During my formative years, I was drawn to television programs like *Dark Shadows,* a daytime drama that featured vampires, ghosts, werewolves, and a variety of monsters, and to sci-fi programs, like *Star Trek* and *The Invaders,* that featured stories about extraterrestrials and UFOs. However, when it came to the paranormal, I found nonfiction to be much more interesting than fiction, and I was constantly on the lookout for books, magazines, and newspaper articles reporting real-life, unexplained phenomenon. To this day, I still have scrapbooks filled with articles that I clipped and saved as a child. There are news stories about UFOs, ghosts, Bigfoot, and a multitude of other strange sightings.

Eventually, to my great delight and satisfaction, I discovered a little magazine called *Fate,* which featured "true reports of the strange and unknown." *Fate* has been around since 1948, and it was probably only a matter of time before I crossed paths with it. Today it is edited and published by Phyllis Galde, but back in those days it was edited by Curtis Fuller. This magazine fulfilled my need for information on these topics, and at the same time exposed me to entirely new mysteries.

Like I said, I was a strange child. In school, if I had to give a speech or write a paper, my topic of choice would be things like UFOs building the pyramids, the ghost of Abraham Lincoln haunting the White House, or Bigfoot roaming the Midwest. Most times, I was marked down because of my choice of topics, and on one occasion, I was given an F.

When I was a teenager, I was recruited into a fundamentalist church, and according to their doctrines, having an interest in the paranormal is anathema. These things were a substitute for God, they said. They told me there was no such thing as the Loch Ness Monster; I pointed out that on more than one occasion the Bible talks about sea monsters (Gen. 1:21; Ps. 74:13; 148:8). They told me there is no such thing as UFOs or ETs; I pointed out that Ezekiel

INTRODUCTIONS

describes four living creatures that descended from the heavens in a vehicle that looked like a bright wheel in the middle of a wheel (Ezek. 1). They told me there is no such thing as ghosts; I pointed out that, according to the Bible, when the disciples of Jesus expressed a belief in ghosts, Jesus neither corrected nor reprimanded them for that belief (Mt. 14:22-27). I quickly learned that in this church they don't like it when you ask too many questions, and they especially don't like it when you know the Bible better than they do. The ministers expected their followers to have blind faith in them and to obey them, but I refused to be credulous and submissive to mere humans. Needless to say, these fundamentalists and I eventually went our separate ways.

Years later, there was an interesting event that changed the direction of my life. My brother Rick and I were visiting a cemetery where our great, great grandparents were buried. George and Eliza Fisk had lived in Minnesota with their twelve children, then moved to Wisconsin via covered wagon and settled there. I took a picture of their gravestone, then asked Rick to take a picture of me standing behind the headstone. Later, I viewed the photo of me by the grave and found that the camera had picked up something unexpected. The image showed what appeared to be a bluish-white mist that seemed to be coming from the grave and surrounding me. At the time the picture was taken there was no mist, smoke, or fog present that could account for the anomaly. I presented the picture to photography and camera experts and none of them could explain the image. I even went so far as to show it to James Randi, the professional skeptic and debunker, and he admitted that even he couldn't explain what was captured by the camera.

This photo renewed my interest in the paranormal and ultimately led me down the road to becoming a paranormal investigator and to investigating the haunted locations of Minnesota as presented in this book.

Some of you might prefer to read this book from the comfort and safety of your own home, and that's fine. But, for those of you who dare, here is your opportunity to check under the bed and to look behind the mysterious door. Sometimes there's nothing there

INTRODUCTIONS

beyond what your imagination and inner fears have created, but in the process of investigation you might learn something about yourself and even conquer those fears. On the other hand, by visiting these haunted locations, you just might have your own paranormal experience that reshapes your perception and understanding of the meaning of death and life.

Best wishes,

Terry Fisk

NORTHEASTERN MINNESOTA

MINNESOTA ROAD GUIDE TO HAUNTED LOCATIONS

40 Club Inn

Location: Aitkin, Aitkin County, Minnesota
Address: 950 2nd St. NW, Aitkin, MN 56431-1151
Phone: (218) 927-2903

Directions: From Aitkin take Highway 410 to the east. The restaurant will be on your right.

Ghost Lore

Often times in life people become emotionally attached to their homes or their places of work. For the booming restaurant just outside of Aitkin, it is not just the living that have become attached to it.

- A man that committed suicide in the upstairs apartment now haunts the place.

1 NORTHEASTERN MINNESOTA

- The jukebox will often turn itself on.
- Strange footsteps are reported throughout the restaurant.
- The staff get negative feelings while working the night shift.

Investigation

In 1999, a man named Tom (last name withheld) did rent the upstairs apartment. When the owners noticed that Tom had not shown up for work, they became worried, as Tom was always a reliable employee. The concerned owners finally went into Tom's apartment to check on him. Inside the apartment they found Tom's dead body. Cuddled up along side of Tom was his dog. The cause of Tom's death was due to a bag of drugs found lodged in his throat. It is not known if the death was an accident or a planned suicide. The apartment is currently empty and the owners have no plans to rent it.

Usually the paranormal events take place late at night after large gatherings or directly after a big party or event.

Many staff reported walking through cold spots in the restaurant. Others have felt a cold breeze eerily pass by them as though someone was there.

1 NORTHEASTERN MINNESOTA

Many times, while working the night shift, staff members will have a negative feeling pass over them.

The owners report that the bar's lights will often flicker on their own and have been known to turn on and off by themselves.

Often times the staff have noticed that the jukebox will turn itself on and start playing music. On one occasion shortly after Tom's death, the jukebox started up and played the same Uncle Kracker song that was played at Tom's funeral. The workers were immediately taken back due to the fact that the song that played was not available in the jukebox.

Late at night, many of the pub's TVs will turn on and off by themselves. Often times the TVs will have only static on the screen.

The radio in the upstairs office will suddenly turn on and start playing when no one is near it.

No visual apparitions have been sighted by the customers or staff.

MINNESOTA ROAD GUIDE TO HAUNTED LOCATIONS

Lakeview Cemetery

Location: Buhl, St. Louis County, Minnesota
Address: Morse Road, Buhl, MN

Directions: From Hwy 169 turn East on Morse Road. Follow the road to the cemetery.

Ghost Lore

When people think of haunted places, cemeteries are often the first thing that comes to mind. Cemeteries have the ability to invoke thoughts of death, fear, and the afterlife. However, many visitors to the secluded Buhl cemetery are reminded that cemeteries are also associated with ghosts.

- Ghostly voices have been recorded by visitors of the cemetery.
- Many young visitors drive out to the cemetery only to experience paranormal events.

1 NORTHEASTERN MINNESOTA

Investigation

Stories of the cemetery have been around for many years, and many residents are familiar with the haunted cemetery.

We spoke with a witness who was out in the cemetery when he noticed someone was locking up the gates. The man thought it was very strange because he had never seen the gates closed. As the witness walked closer, he noticed that the "man" he was watching was dressed in clothes from the 1920s. The strange man walked across the road and then disappeared. Upon further investigation, the man found that the old gate was broken and would not even close.

Several investigators claim to have recorded a mysterious voice telling them about a flag in the cemetery. This group also states that while all the other flags in the cemetery were absolutely still, one flag was moving on its own.

A psychic woman told the *Hibbing Daily Tribune* that she believes that people have upset the spirits of Lakeview Cemetery.

MINNESOTA ROAD GUIDE TO HAUNTED LOCATIONS

1 NORTHEASTERN MINNESOTA

Bertha's Grave

Location: Coleraine, Itasca County, Minnesota
Address: Lakeside Cemetery, Crooked Rd., Coleraine, MN

Directions: From Highway 169 turn onto 10 West. From 10 West turn onto Crooked Road. The cemetery will be on the right hand side.

Ghost Lore

If you think the idea of spending your life alone is depressing, imagine having to spend your afterlife alone. That is exactly what is said to have happened to a witch buried in Lakeside Cemetery.

- The grave of a witch is hidden in the cemetery.
- Her headstone is said to move around, and the headstone is not visible on Halloween.

- An apparition of a woman has been spotted roaming through the cemetery.

History

The sign at the cemetery states that the cemetery is Trout Lake Cemetery even though the official name of the cemetery is Lakeside.

The headstone of the alleged witch is that of Bertha Maynard, who was born January 26th, 1872, and died on January 27th, 1910.

According to the Northern Minnesota Paranormal Investigators (NMPI), the story of Bertha has been around since at least the 1920's. They found no evidence that Bertha was a witch.

Investigation

The NMPI also found that Bertha's grave sits alone on the bottom of the hill due to the fact that her family did not want her grave moved when all the other graves were relocated. The other graves in the cemetery were relocated to the top of the cemetery to avoid the frequent flooding that takes place in the lower section of the cemetery.

Bertha's grave was indeed missing for seven years. It was removed by the cemetery caretaker because of the frequent vandalism that occurred in the cemetery. The stone was finally replaced at the request of Bertha's family.

Bertha's headstone was visible when we investigated the cemetery, and it remained stationary the whole time.

Several ghostly voices have been recorded on audio tape throughout the cemetery. These EVPs are believed to be from Bertha.

MINNESOTA ROAD GUIDE TO HAUNTED LOCATIONS

Photo courtesy of Brian Leffler of NMPI.

Photo courtesy of Brian Leffler of NMPI.

1 NORTHEASTERN MINNESOTA

Strange apparitions of a female spirit have been spotted in the cemetery. It is not known if these ghostly sightings were that of Bertha.

Photo courtesy of Brian Leffler of NMPI.

MINNESOTA ROAD GUIDE TO HAUNTED LOCATIONS

Charlie's Club

Location: Duluth, St. Louis County, Minnesota
Address: 5527 Grand Ave., Duluth, MN 55807-2537
Phone: (715) 335-4451

Directions: Take exit #251A/Cody Street onto Cody Street. Turn right on N Central Ave. Bear right on Grand Ave. and arrive at Charlie's Club.

Ghost Lore

This blue-collar bar has a small town feel to it, as many of the patrons know one another and are quick to make a stranger feel welcome. While Charlie's Club may appear like a normal bar from the outside, the building's history may prove to house more spirits than the kind you drink.

- Haunted by an old woman who only reveals herself to men.

- The spirit of a recently deceased patron still inhabits the saloon looking for one last drink.

- The bar was a former brothel and the ghosts of former 'ladies' still stick around to entertain the men.

- Many items in the bar get mysteriously moved, seemingly on their own.

History

The complete history of the bar is still unknown. The complete building may be older than the assessor's records indicate.

1909 – The building was constructed as a saloon and house of ill repute. The original building consisted of four floors. The building was a well known speak easy in the area and was reported to have a brothel employing many girls.

1916 – The building was rebuilt as a single story building. The four-story building did burn down and it is thought that this new construction was to re-build the bar.

1980-90s – The bar was called The Modern.

1995 – The bar was purchased by Vickie Haugland. The bar was already aptly named Charlie's Club, after former owner Charlie Lemon.

2006 – On May 22nd, Charlie's Club was destroyed by fire. None of the patrons or employees were harmed.

1 NORTHEASTERN MINNESOTA

Investigation

We spoke with the bartender, Jimmy, who stated that his family has owned the bar for nearly 30 years.

Many of the patrons refer to the ghost as 'Sadie.' How the ghost came to be known as Sadie is uncertain.

A female bartender stated that while she was busy working one evening, she glimpsed the ghost of a man out of the corner of her eye. Although she got a good look at the ghost, he soon disappeared.

A DJ was setting up his equipment for the night when he heard the back door open on its own. Knowing that the door is extremely difficult to open, he checked who was entering the bar, yet when he investigated, no one was found and the door was still shut and locked.

An employee was in the back kitchen putting away groceries when he spotted what appeared to be a ghost of a woman out of the corner of his eye. When he quickly turned to look at her, she had disappeared right before his eyes.

While working one evening, a new female bartender saw what she thought was a man sitting by the beer taps enjoying a cold drink. However, when she described the man to others in the bar, they told her that she saw the ghost of Boogie. Boogie was a regular at the bar who had passed away just a few weeks prior to the woman's sighting. The location of the ghost was the chair in which Boogie always sat.

A janitor reported on many nights that his cleaning equipment would be re-arranged by some unseen force.

Patrons have reported feeling someone bump them or push them a bit while they are engaged in a game of pool.

Staff have reported hearing the eerie sounds of the bathroom doors opening and slamming while no one is in the bar.

At this time, it is not known if they will rebuild Charlie's Club.

Glensheen Mansion

Location: Duluth, St. Louis County, Minnesota
Address: 3300 London Rd., Duluth, MN 55804-3735
Phone: (218) 726-8910

Ghost Lore

The Congdon Estate is perhaps the most recognized home in Minnesota. Even though the mansion tries to play down its past, the mystery of the murders that took place in the home only grows. If a traumatic death does cause one to become a ghost, then the Glensheen is certainly on the top of the list of haunted places.

- The mansion is haunted by two women who were murdered in the home.

- Mysterious apparitions have been seen roaming through the estate.

1 NORTHEASTERN MINNESOTA

- Strange noises have been reported in the historic mansion.

History

Chester Congdon grew up in a very poor family. However, Chester was able to go to college, where he met his future wife Clara. Chester eventually became a lawyer, and by the age of 47 was Minnesota's second richest man.

1905-1908 – Chester Congdon built his 7.6-acre English Country estate in the heavily wooded lakeside area of Duluth. His main house was constructed with Neo-Jacobean style arches. At a price of $854,000, the home was one of the finest in all of Minnesota.

1908 – The Congdons move into their new home.

1977 – Before her death, Elisabeth Congdon bequeathed the mansion to the University of Minnesota. Elisabeth feared that her heirs were unable to take over the costs of running the home.

1977 – Elisabeth Congdon and her nurse, Velma Pietila were murdered in the home. Elisabeth's daughter Marjorie, and her husband Roger Caldwell, were arrested on charges of murder.

1978 – Elisabeth's son in law, Roger, was convicted of the two murders.

1978 – Elisabeth's daughter Marjorie, was found not guilty of the murders. In a strange twist after the case, the jury throws a party and actually invites Marjorie.

1979 – The Congdon estate was opened to the public as a museum.

1982 – Roger was given a new trial. He was released from prison after serving five years.

Investigation

Two murders did indeed take place in the estate. Investigative reporter Joe Kimball wrote in his book, *Secrets of the Congdon Mansion,* that 84-year-old Elisabeth Congdon, who was partially paralyzed, was smothered to death with a pillow while her nurse, Velma Pietila, was bludgeoned to death with a candlestick holder on the grand staircase.

After her trial, Marjorie was involved with several more mysterious cases, including the death of her second husband, Wally Hagen.

We spoke with several staff that have seen ghostly shadows while working in the home.

One employee was working high up on a ladder when he felt someone pulling at his ankles. Thinking that it was impossible for someone to have climbed up the ladder behind him, he quickly spun around to find that no one was there.

For years the tour guides would try to hide the murders and downplay the negative events that took place at the mansion. Even today, you may have a hard time getting some guides to discuss the ghosts of the mansion.

Visitors touring the mansion report getting an eerie feeling when viewing the area where the murders took place.

1 NORTHEASTERN MINNESOTA

Heritage House

Location: Embarrass, Saint Louis County, Minnesota

Directions: From Highway 21 in Embarrass, turn on Salo Road. You will pass by the Heritage Campground. The heritage home is the next driveway to your left. The bridge is just down the road.

Ghost Lore

A lot of great scary stories revolve around an old abandoned house somewhere out in the country. These general stories are often told with as little specific information as possible to make them as universal as possible. The main goal of the story is to create fear in the mind of the reader. However, the legends become much scarier when the old abandoned house is actually real. Such is the case with the heritage home.

The ghost of a young boy that was drowned by his abusive father in the nearby river haunts the bridge where he died. It is said that the father told him Jesus could walk on water and he should be able to too.

History

1902 – Mikko Pyhala immigrated into the United States from Finland.

1909 – The Pyhala family purchased the land in Embarrass.

1916 – Young William Pyhala, drowned in the Embarrass River.

1924 – The last of seventeen children was born.

Investigation

The bridge does pass over a small stream that was a favorite fishing hole of the family. William, one of the Pyhala's young children, did drown in the Embarrass River in 1916. However, we found no

1 NORTHEASTERN MINNESOTA

evidence that the father had anything to do with the death.

Several of the family members still live in the area.

We spoke with a witness who reported hearing strange noises while walking down near the Embarrass River.

Several people have reported seeing the ghost of a young boy lurking near the Embarrass River. Most believe that it is indeed the ghost of William Pyhala.

Note: The Heritage House is private property.

MINNESOTA ROAD GUIDE TO HAUNTED LOCATIONS

Hoyt Lakes Memorial Cemetery

Location: Hoyt Lakes, Saint Louis County, Minnesota
Address: Hampshire Dr., Hoyt Lakes, MN 55750

Directions: From Kennedy turn left onto Hampshire Dr. and the cemetery is on the right side of the road.

Ghost Lore

- A young girl was frightened to death in the cemetery after being left by her friends.

- Those who pass through the cemetery see the ghost of a young woman waiting for her ride home.

Investigation

We found numerous graves of young women in the cemetery that could fit the description of this case including:

   Linda Wandrus 1950-1969
   Darlene Bobart 1951-1969

However, if a young woman was left behind in the graveyard by her friends, they would have no idea how she died. If she did indeed die of fright there would be no one there to witness it.

Many stories from cemeteries around the world tell the story of a young girl waiting for a ride. The most common of these stories is the "Vanishing Hitchhiker" that often involves a young woman seeking a ride to a dance, a ride home, or just simply a ride with no destination.

This case is still pending.

MINNESOTA ROAD GUIDE TO HAUNTED LOCATIONS

Haunted Train Trestles

Location: The Willard Munger State Trail, Moose Lake, Carlton County, Minnesota

Directions: Follow Arrowhead Lane-Highway 61 to Kasper Road. Turn on Kasper Road, park your car, and walk to the Willard Munger recreation trail. Once on the trail, turn right for approximately 100 yards until you get to the old bridge. This is the old train trestle.

Ghost Lore

The small town of Moose Lake has its fair share of tragic history, as the town was nearly wiped out in the great fire of 1918. Tucked away in this sleepy town is the story of the ghost of an old Native American woman who haunts the site of her murder.

1 NORTHEASTERN **MINNESOTA**

31

Many users of the walking trail have seen the ghost of a woman who appears on the old railroad trestle.

Many people report seeing the ghosts of others in the area, possibly the spirits of those who perished in the 1918 fire.

History

The Willard Munger State Trail stretches 72 miles from Hinckley to Duluth making it the nation's longest paved multi-use trail.

Train Trestle. In 1889, Jim Coffee, a Native American, had spent the better part of the day in the town's saloons. According to David Anderson's book, *Moose Lake Area History,* after spending the day drinking, Jim decided to begin his long venture home along the railroad tracks. His mother, Sally Coffee met him a short distance from town on the tracks over Moose Horn River. Sally's murderer shot her in the head and left her dead body on the tracks. Her body was discovered by the engineer of a passing train. He immediately notified the village officers. The section crew transported her

1 NORTHEASTERN MINNESOTA

body to the old train depot. Jim Coffee was quickly apprehended and brought to court where he denied all of the charges against him. The court had no witnesses to the murder and was forced to release him.

1918 Fire. In 1918, Minnesota was hit with a monstrous fire that turned out to be one of the greatest disasters in the state's history. On October 12, 1918, an out of control fire burned numerous communities of northeastern MN, including Moose Lake. Over 450 people died during the fire. A 27-foot monument directly north of town was erected at the site of the mass grave that houses the victims of the fire. You are able to get to the monument by following the trail past the bridge.

Investigation

We spoke with the Moose Lake Historical Society whose headquarters are in the old depot building where Sally's body was brought. They were familiar with the story, yet they had not reported any strange activity in the building.

It should be noted that the trail in which the haunted tracks are on also leads to the 1918 monument and mass grave of those who lost their lives in the great fire of 1918.

1 NORTHEASTERN **MINNESOTA**

Warden's House

Location: Stillwater, Washington County, Minnesota
Address: 602 Main St. N., Stillwater, MN 55082-4010
Phone: (612) 439-5956
Open May through October

Directions: Take Main Street in Stillwater

Ghost Lore

- The Warden's House is said to be home to three ghosts.
- Ghosts of former prisoners are still serving their time at the warden's former home.
- Staff report cold chills and feelings of eeriness in the home.
- Passersby report seeing someone in the house when it is suppose to be empty.

- Visitors report strange happenings while touring the home.

History

The Warden's House Museum is located next to the former site of the Minnesota Territorial Prison. During the 1800's and early 1900's, the prison housed some of Minnesota's most notorious criminals including James, Robert, and Cole Younger of the Jesse James Gang. The bank-robbing brothers were model prisoners and eventually released on good behavior. The home itself contains 14 rooms that are decorated with numerous items from the time period.

1853 – The Warden's House Museum was constructed as the residence of the Minnesota Territorial Prison warden.

1853-1914 – The house served as the home of 13 different Wardens.

1 NORTHEASTERN MINNESOTA

1914 – The prison was moved to the city of Bayport, where it still stands.

1914 – A deputy warden still used the Warden's House.

1941 – The State of Minnesota sold the home to the Washington County Historical Society.

1941 – The Washington County Historical Society opened the house as a museum.

1974 – The house was placed on the National Register of Historic Places.

Investigation

Many psychics have reported feeling the ghost of a young woman upstairs in the 'baby' room. They often report that she is with a young child or is desperately searching for her baby. Many different psychics refer to her as 'Trudy.' The psychics may be speaking about Gertrude (Trudy), the daughter of former warden Henry

Wolfer. Gertrude was the youngest of the warden's four children and was the only girl. At the age of 21, Gertrude fell in love with Dr. Winslow Chambers, a new employee at the prison.

Gertrude and Winslow were married in Stillwater, and on November 4th, 1907, they had a baby boy named Winston. Eight months later, at the age of 23, Gertrude died suddenly of appendicitis. Their newborn son Winston was moved back into the Warden's House with his grandparents.

We spoke with a guide who informed us that many of the guides at the home get a creepy feeling while entering the master bedroom, and often like to spend the least amount of time in this room during the tour.

While walking from the 'baby' room to the master bedroom, a visitor reported feeling a burst of cold air on her neck.

One intern reported hearing a mysterious humming in the house. Although she thoroughly investigated the noise, she was unable to locate the source.

1 NORTHEASTERN MINNESOTA

Several visitors report seeing a wandering ghost of a man. This ghost is also said to be wearing a dark or gray prison suit.

One evening some visitors were outside admiring the house when they looked up the long set of steps next to the home and noticed a man in a gray prison suit walking up the steps. They just stopped and looked at him, and he stopped and stared at them and then disappeared. When they got to the top of the stairs, the man was no where to be found.

Next door to the Warden's House, several condominiums are being constructed. One day while working on the condominiums, several of the workers thought they saw a woman in the window and called the staff to report it. The staff informed the workers that no one had been in the house that day.

In the basement, several psychics report seeing the ghost of a man in a gray prison suit. Some psychics have claimed that the man was shoveling coal, even though the house was never heated with coal. However, only model prisoners that were classified as 1st grade or 1st class wore gray prison suits. Many trusted prisoners would be allowed to work in the Warden's House as cooks, maids, caretakers.

1 NORTHEASTERN MINNESOTA

Water Street Inn

Location: Stillwater, Washington County, Minnesota
Address: 101 Water St. S., Stillwater, MN 55082-5150
Phone: (561) 439-6000
Fax: (651) 430-9393
Website: www.waterstreetinn.us

Directions: From Main Street turn east into Water Street.

Ghost Lore

Nestled along the St. Croix River is the historic Lumber Barons Exchange Building. In 1890, the building housed several businesses and a saloon. One hundred and ten years later, the building still houses a saloon and it has added a ghost or two.

- A military man passed away after a drunken stupor on the second floor. His body odor can still be detected today.

MINNESOTA ROAD GUIDE TO HAUNTED LOCATIONS

- Many visitors report seeing strange ghostly sights while at the Inn.
- The building is also referred to as Lumber Barons.

History

1890 – Stillwater's Lumber Barons constructed the Lumber Exchange Building. The building was constructed by the Union Depot and Transfer Company. The building had top secure vaults that housed the wealth of many of Stillwater's most affluent residents. Barbers, a post office, and a saloon were some of the first businesses in the building.

1900-1910 – The building was used by various businesses including insurance companies, lawyers, and real estate companies. The change in occupants is largely due to the rapid decline in the lumber business that swept through the country.

1960 – The Hooleys moved their offices into the Lumber Exchange Building. The buildings were also renovated at this time.
1994 – The Minnesota Historical Society and the National Trust worked to restore the building to its original luster.

1995 – The Water Street Inn opened to the public.

Investigation

We were unable to find any death record of a confederate soldier. However, many saloons of the time attracted shady characters and someone drinking themselves to death would not have been too outlandish to believe.

The new pub is located in the same spot as the original saloon. We spoke with several employees who have not had a personal experience, yet had heard of the hauntings of the young man. One employee stated that he had heard from several guests that while they were staying at the Inn, they reported that they thought they had seen the ghost of a young man.

Staff reported hearing strange noises while working the evenings at the inn. One staff member informed us that he had smelled the strong scent of body odor while working. No source was ever found for the odor.

1 NORTHEASTERN **MINNESOTA**

Old Jail Bed & Breakfast

Location: Taylors Falls, Chisago County, Minnesota
Address: 349 W. Government St., Taylors Falls, MN 55084-1157
Phone: (651) 465-3112
Website: www.oldjail.com

Directions: From US 8 take a right on Bench Street to Ravine Street. At Ravine Street turn left and it will turn into Government Street.

Ghost Lore

Never has spending a night in jail sounded more appealing than it does at the Old Jail Bed and Breakfast. A rare find in the US, this B&B allows you to spend the night in an authentic old jailhouse. Complete with the original iron door that many "visitors" peered out, the jail now comes with all the modern conveniences that make

B&Bs so popular. Immediately the history of the building seeps in and one cannot help but to be transported back to a time when handcuffs and chairs filled the jail. It is also here that many people believe that the ghosts of several inmates are still waiting for parole.

- Strange noises have been reported with no known cause.
- Several former visitors of the jail are said to have stayed.

History

If history is what you are looking for then the Old Jail B&B is a perfect place for you. While running a successful brewery on Angel Hill, Frank and Joseph Schottmuller decided to construct a building on Government Street, to be used as a saloon. The benefit of this building was that it also contained a cave in which the brothers used to store their brew. However the brothers wanted some additional living space, so they purchased an old 1851 two-story stable from the Chisago House Hotel. Al Kunz, in his article,

"From Barn to Bed & Breakfast," states that a fire in 1902 burned most of the buildings in town, yet the stable was untouched. The brothers placed the old stable directly on top of the saloon and made it their permanent residence. Kunz also states that the saloon was then known as the Cave Saloon and was run by Peter Trump. In 1884, the town jailhouse was ironically constructed right next door to the saloon, making it a short trip for those coming from the saloon. The cost of the jail was $311.76 and of that money, Swen Olsen, the carpenter, received $51.80 but he had to supply the wood stove and $36.26 was paid to the blacksmith for the iron doors. The jailhouse originally contained four jail cells and was constructed by stacking 2X4s on top of one another. According to Jean, one of the innkeepers, and a local historian, this unique construction was done with the belief that it would be harder for the inmates to break out.

Having over 200 different entries on the abstract, the property has served as numerous businesses throughout the years including a beauty shop, a general store, and a mortuary.

Investigation

While sleeping, a couple staying at the Old Jail House felt their cat jump up onto their bed. However, they had not brought a cat with them, yet both felt the indentation of a cat jumping up on the bed.

One woman awoke at 4 am and went down the steps to use the restroom. While on the stairs, the woman saw a glowing light. Not sure if she was imagining it, she continued on to the bathroom. She was a bit surprised to see that the glow continued to follow her. She then stopped and looked at the glow, which materialized into an old woman and little boy staring intently at her. She tried to scream but no sound came out of her mouth. She then heard the ghost of the little boy say, "Miss, don't be afraid, we are here to watch over you." The woman closed her eyes and when she reopened them, both the old woman and the little boy were gone.

1 NORTHEASTERN MINNESOTA

Black Woods Restaurant

Location: Two Harbors, Lake County, Minnesota
Address: 612 7th Ave., Two Harbors, MN 55616-1454
Phone: (218) 834-3846
Website: www.blackwoodsrestaurants.com

Directions: Follow Hwy 61 to 7th Ave. The restaurant will be on your right.

Ghost Lore

- The restaurant is haunted by a mysterious lady in white.
- Servers feel the chill of ghostly breath on their body.
- Many items are often re-arranged by some unseen force.
- Servers will hear phantom footsteps in the restaurant when no one is around.

History

As you leisurely drive along beautifully scenic Highway 61, you will pass many shops unique to the area, yet the most unique shop may be the haunted Black Woods Restaurant. The restaurant opened in 1994 in Two Harbors, and currently has four locations throughout MN.

Investigation

Employees have reported seeing the ghost of a young woman wearing a long white gown throughout the restaurant. This woman often disappears right into thin air.

We spoke with several employees who clearly heard footsteps in the restaurant but were unable to trace their source.

A former bookkeeper felt the ghost follow her home one evening. As her husband was lying in bed by himself, he felt a depression in the bed as though someone had crawled in next to him. Assuming it was he wife, he turned over to say hello and was surprised to find no one was there.

1 NORTHEASTERN MINNESOTA

We spoke with several waitresses who were working at the restaurant when they felt the chill of someone breathing on their shoulder.

A former cleaning lady sighted the ghost on numerous occasions. On one occasion the air around her got eerily cold and the woman saw the ghost of a young girl walk down the hall. The ghost appeared to swipe her hand across one of the tables.

A cleaning lady had just finished arranging the coat rack hangers when she looked back to find that they had all been pushed to the side by some unseen force.

A waiter who was in the restaurant by himself heard footsteps coming up behind him. A bit startled, he quickly spun around to find that there was no one there.

NORTHWESTERN MINNESOTA

MINNESOTA ROAD GUIDE TO HAUNTED LOCATIONS

Old Broadway

Location: Alexandria, Douglas County, Minnesota
Official Name: Old Broadway Food & Spirits
Address: 319 Broadway St., Alexandria, MN 56308-1418
Phone: (320) 763-3999

Ghost Lore

- The building was the site of an old morgue.
- The building was once the town's brothel.
- This former brothel is haunted by many of the women who 'worked' in the house.
- During evenings, both staff and customers have reported seeing a female ghost walking around on the second floor dining area.

- The ghost of a woman has been spotted in the numerous mirrors of the restaurant by staff and customers.

History

This civil war era large Victorian-looking building was constructed in 1866 by William E. Hicks. Mr. Hicks acquired the land through H.T. Wells who owned the land from 1862-1866. Hicks served as the financial editor for the New York Evening Post before moving to Minnesota. Hicks constructed the building to be used for his home. Hicks is also credited with starting the community's first newspaper, aptly named *The Alexandria Post.*

By 1926, the building was being used as a funeral home. The building housed the Carlson Funeral Home from 1926 through 1929. By the time of the Great Depression in 1929, the house once again became a private residence. It remained a private residence for many years, yet plagued by neglect and vandalism, it slowly started to fall into disrepair and was vacant and dilapidated by the 1980s.

In 1986, the historic home was once again converted, this time into a restaurant called The Bronc's on Broadway.

On July 19, 1993, the building was sold and re-named Old Broadway.

In May of 2004, the restaurant was purchased by the owners of Simply Tasteful.

Investigation

We spoke with several employees that had not had a personal experience, yet were familiar with previous employees' stories. While they were working, former employees reported seeing the ghost of a woman who looked as though she was from a different time period.

Several former staff also reported seeing what they believed was a ghost of a woman in many of the restaurant's mirrors. When they turned around to get a better look at the woman, they found that no one was there.

Most of the reported sightings came from the second floor and from the staircase connecting the first and second floors.

The staff did confirm that the ghost that is reported to haunt the restaurant is a female.

Many of the staff could not say as to whether the building was ever a brothel. Local historians at the historical society did state that the house was once an "unofficial" brothel. Most brothels of the time-period were considered "unofficial" and would not show up on the property deed or in the normal history of the building.

The current staff also reported that during closing time many of the employees are afraid to go upstairs to the second floor to shut off the lights and lock up. They report getting an eerie feeling while upstairs all alone.

2 NORTHWESTERN MINNESOTA

MINNESOTA ROAD GUIDE TO HAUNTED LOCATIONS

2 NORTHWESTERN MINNESOTA

Thayer's Historic Bed n' Breakfast

Location: Annandale, Wright County, Minnesota
Address: 60 Elm St. W., Annandale, MN 55302
Phone: (320) 274-8222
Website: www.thayers.net

Ghost Lore

Often people are searching for a haunted place to spend the evening. Most people who stay at a B&B are adventurous folk searching for something a little bit different than the typical chain hotels. If you are looking for some fun and excitement and possibly a ghost experience, Thayer's is most definitely for you.

Upon arriving in the quaint little town, two things stick out to you. First is the B&B itself. The Old West Victorian building has a welcoming effect. The second thing you notice is the warm friendliness of your host Sharon Gammell. Sharon owns the B&B and also happens to be a psychic who has been giving readings for nearly 45 years. After only a few minutes of talking with her, you will see why the B&B is so popular.

- Ghosts of cats still roam around the house.
- Staff have seen the ghost of a man wandering around the home.
- Doors will mysteriously open and close on their own.
- A server was bringing out a heavy tray of food when the door suddenly opened by itself to let her pass through.
- Staff and guests often hear mysterious knocks on doors and on the walls.
- The original owners often pop in to visit the guests.

History

1895 – The building was constructed as a railroad hotel. The hotel was built by Gus and Caroline Thayer with funding from the Soo Line Railroad Company. The property was constructed in the Victorian style complete with a Gentleman's Parlor and many of the popular adornments of the time period.

1895 – Thayer's New Hotel opened. Housing both railroad employees and tourists, the hotel was one of the finest places to spend the evening in the whole Midwest.

1900s – The hotel remained a popular place for those seeking rest and recreation.

Currently the property is Thayer's Historic Bed n' Breakfast. It is listed on the National Register of Historic Places. Thayer's has also been voted Property of the Year and is ranked among the nation's best B&Bs offering murder mystery dinners.

MINNESOTA ROAD GUIDE TO HAUNTED LOCATIONS

Investigation

We spoke with the owner who informed us that both Gus and Caroline Thayer still visit the historic B&B. Sharon reported that all of the ghosts of Thayer's are friendly and will only visit if the guest asks them to.

An employee complained to the owner that she had not seen a ghost in all the time she had worked at the B&B. Sharon informed her that if she wanted to see a ghost, all she had to do was ask them. About a month after asking to see a ghost, the woman saw the ghost of a man walk directly into a wall. This particular ghost has been seen often at the B&B, and is dubbed the 'worker' as he is always dressed in work bibs.

Both Gus and Caroline Thayer have been spotted by both guests and staff. Gus is known to leave pennies for the guests in many of the rooms.

2 NORTHWESTERN MINNESOTA

At special events and parties many guests and staff report seeing a little girl sitting on the staircase as though she is vigilantly watching over people.

The B&B also is home to three ghost cats that are spotted regularly throughout the B&B.

A four-year-old boy was in the house with his mother who was picking up a gift certificate. He and his older brother asked if they could go upstairs. When they returned downstairs, the four-year-old curiously asked the owner how many cats were in the home. The owner told the young boy that there were two cats in the home. The boy looked puzzled, and again went upstairs. Upon his second return, he told the owner that he saw a third cat on the third floor. He described the cat as being big, fluffy, and brown. He also said the cat's name was Coco and that the cat told him to say hello. Coco was one of the owner's cats that had passed away.

A couple that were regular guests of the B&B, reported a strange odor coming from upstairs and told Sharon about it. The couple then went out for the evening, and when they came back, the owner told them that it was a new ghost in the home and that she had taken care of the problem. The couple was extremely skeptical, even through they had stayed at Thayer's often, they did not believe in ghosts and started poking fun at the ghost. When the couple was in bed for the evening the lights turned on, and the room got really cold. It was at that moment that they saw a ghost of a man at the end of their bed. The ghost tipped his hat toward them and then simply disappeared. The couple was so shaken, that they left that very night. It should be noted that the couple has since been back to the B&B.

One guest reported that her room inexplainably filled with the scent of a peculiar pipe smoke. She believed that this was the ghost of her deceased uncle who always smoked the same flavor of tobacco when he was alive.

One couple was staying in Ms. Amy's room, when they noticed one of the house cats stretched out on its back playing. They thought that the view of the cat would make an interesting photo. However, when they got their photos back, they were shocked to find four spirits in the picture with the cat.

2 NORTHWESTERN **MINNESOTA**

Billy's Bar and Grill

Location: Anoka, Anoka County, Minnesota
Address: 214 Jackson St., Anoka, MN 55303-2211
Phone: (763) 421-3570

Directiosn: From Highway 14 turn north on East Main Street. Turn west on Jackson Street.

Ghost Lore

The restaurant was once a brothel and is still haunted by several of the 'ladies' that were employed there. Mrs. Jackson was the madam of the house and ran an unofficial brothel out of the hotel. Eventually the patrons got greedy and killed her to take the profits of the ladies.

Another version of the story is that Mrs. Jackson became so distressed about losing the hotel that she hanged herself from one of the chandeliers on the third floor.

MINNESOTA ROAD GUIDE TO HAUNTED LOCATIONS

- The ghost of a woman haunts the upstairs window where she committed suicide.
- If you travel by the restaurant in the evening, you will see a shadowy figure in the window.
- Staff and visitors report pictures moving.
- The ghost has been seen moving around the restaurant.

History

1848 – Charles G. Jackson was born in Sweden.

1854 – Lotta C. Iverson was born in Christiana, Norway.

1866 – Charles moved to St. Paul.

1870s – Mr. Jackson moved to Anoka.

1877 – Lotta married Mr. C.G. Jackson in St. Paul.

1877 – Mr. Jackson built and opened the Anoka Hotel.

1880s – The Anoka Hotel changed its name to the Jackson Hotel.

1884 – The Jackson Hotel burned in the great August fire.

1885 – The new hotel was opened in its current location at the cost of $6,000.

1885 – The first murder took place in Anoka city limits outside the Jackson Hotel.

1904 – Major renovations were done to the hotel costing $7,000.

1918 – Mrs. Jackson died of pneumonia.

1927 – The Jackson Hotel was willed to Fred Jackson.

1952 – The hotel's restaurant and bar closed down. The area was converted into apartments.

1975 – The building was closed down. Fred sold the building to Mrs. Delong.

1979 – The building was placed on the National Register of Historic Places.

1987 – Wayne Meloche purchased the hotel.

Currently – The building houses Billy's Bar and Grill.

Investigation

We spoke with several historians who confirmed that the hotel was used as an unofficial bordello as most hotels of the time were.

The hotel was a very popular place for loggers of the area. The men would spend all month working long hours in the lumber camp saving all of their money. At the end of the month, the loggers

MINNESOTA ROAD GUIDE TO HAUNTED LOCATIONS

would excitedly venture into town to stay at the luxury hotel for the weekend. The loggers used this time to relax and unwind from the hard work of the logging camp. In fact, they relaxed so much that they would spend their entire month's paycheck in just one weekend at the hotel. This money was spent evenly on the room, drinks, and women. When their weekend was over, the loggers would head back into the woods to work at the lumber camps for another month, only to repeat the process all over again.

Mrs. Jackson did not die in the hotel, nor was she murdered in the hotel. In fact, she and her husband moved out to their cottage along Crooked Lake long before her death. Mrs. Jackson died of pneumonia in 1918.

However, one confirmed murder did occur at the Jackson Hotel. It was the first murder in Anoka's city limit. It took place in 1885, as W.F. Mirick murdered Peter Gross outside of the Jackson Hotel. The case was a great mystery at the time, as a motive for the slaying was never discovered. The Anoka County Union reported that local resident William Mirick had spent the evening on a heavy drinking binge. For some unknown reason, Mirick traveled home to retrieve his revolver from his wife. With his revolver in hand, Mirick wandered back into town and continued his drinking. While leaving a tavern, Mirick noticed Peter Gross standing outside the Jackson Hotel. Witnesses stated that they saw Gross and Mirick talking and laughing. Gross apparently said something to Mirick about his going home. Several unknown words were exchanged between the men when Mirick fired a shot at Gross from his Smith and Wesson. Realizing that Mirick was trying to kill him, Gross began to run from the area when Mirick fired another shot into Gross' back. Gross made it into the hotel where a doctor was summoned. Meanwhile police quickly disarmed Mirick and put him in custody. The doctor noticed that Gross was in terrible condition and sent for a priest. Nearly 20 hours later, Gross died in the upstairs of the hotel due to internal bleeding. At the murder trial, Mirick was found guilty.

In the third floor window many visitors and residents report seeing a woman staring down at them. In a strange event, the owners found an empty coffin on the third floor. However, the third floor is currently being used for storage and few people ever go up to it.

One former resident of the Jackson Hotel reported that on many occasions he would hear mysterious noises throughout the rooms.

We spoke with several staff who reported seeing the apparition of a women walking through the restaurant.

Other staff swore that they had witnessed the paintings on the wall move on their own.

MINNESOTA ROAD GUIDE TO HAUNTED LOCATIONS

Cal's Corner Restaurant

Location: Anoka, Anoka County, Minnesota
Address: 1918 1st Ave., Anoka, MN 55303-2437
Phone: (763) 712-0824

Ghost Lore

Anoka is the Halloween capital of the United States, so it is only fitting that ghosts still haunt the community. Although the small unassuming eatery on the corner of town is not filled with pumpkins and other Halloween decorations, it certainly is filled with numerous paranormal events.

- Doors are locked and unlocked by some unseen force.
- The restaurant is on a Native American burial ground.
- Customers report hearing strange noises while eating in the restaurant.

History

- There is much speculation that the restaurant is built on Native American burial ground. We were unable to substantiate this claim.

- The building itself was constructed in 1888.

- Throughout the years, the building has been used for various businesses. One long time resident remembered coming by the building as a child to pick up milk from the basement.

- The building also once housed a shoe store.

- Many restaurants have also passed through the building including the River Front, D Eatery, RNB's, Cully's, and several others.

Investigation

We spoke with the current owner of the restaurant who informed us that he has owned the place for three years, yet he had heard stories of mysterious events happening to previous owners dating back many years.

The owner reported that many times he will close the restaurant for the evening by locking the door and shutting off all the lights. Yet to his amazement, when he returns in the morning, the front door is unlocked and the lights are turned on.

One evening the owner was alone in the store and was down in the basement when he heard what sounded like young girls talking to each other. The owner was positive that the voices were coming from a locked storage area. The owner did not unlock the door to see what was in there.

One day while cooking, an employee felt as though something was next to him on the cooking line. The next thing he knew, something had untied his apron strings.

Customers often report hearing strange noises coming from the downstairs while eating in the restaurant. These sounds have never been explained.

One female employee held a group séance downstairs. While downstairs, the group thought they heard someone walking around upstairs. When they came up to investigate, no one was in the building, but the Christmas tree lights had mysteriously turned on by themselves.

Many customers and staff also report hearing the sounds of a cat coming from the downstairs, yet no cats are ever found in the building.

One evening, after setting up the restaurant for the following day's breakfast, the waitress closed up the restaurant. When she returned the next morning, all of the silverware and salt and pepper shakers were stacked onto one table.

2 NORTHWESTERN **MINNESOTA**

Durkin's Irish Pub

Location: Anoka, Anoka County, Minnesota
Address: 227 E. Main St., Anoka, MN 55303-2402
Phone: (763) 712-0476
Hours: 10 am - 1 am daily

Directions: From Highway 169 turn east on East Main Street and arrive at the pub.

Ghost Lore

The Irish are often times associated with leprechauns, Guinness, and really cool accents. However, many visitors to this Irish pub associate it with ghosts and paranormal happenings.

- The place had so much paranormal activity that an exorcism was performed.

- Many electrical problems are reported.
- Doors inexplainably open and close without the aid of a person.
- Unknown footsteps are often heard throughout the bar.

History

1924 – The building was constructed.

1939 – The bar was called the Idle Hour.

1940-1990s – The building housed numerous other bars throughout the years.

2000 – The bar became Durkin's Irish Pub.

Investigation

The owner and staff believe that all of the ghosts that haunt the pub are friendly in nature.

2 NORTHWESTERN MINNESOTA

Often times when the pub is closed, the owner will be downstairs working when all of a sudden he will hear someone walking around upstairs. Yet, when he looks at the security camera showing the upstairs, no one is there.

The owner did have a person come perform an exorcism in the fall of 2002. The woman said that five ghosts haunted the old pub. The woman also claimed to have allowed the 'good' ghosts to stay at the pub.

For two years, a female customer would come into the pub, sit alone, and talk to herself. After the exorcism was performed, the woman came in, sat down, and asked where the ghost had gone. The staff then discovered that the woman was a self-proclaimed witch, and told them that for the previous two years she had been speaking to a ghost in the pub.

While working at the pub, one of the servers witnessed a coffee mug fly across the room and break on the floor. This event was also witnessed by two patrons of the pub.

A female bartender went to grab some towels when all of the equipment flew off of the top shelf.

The owner reports that the pub has many electrical problems including the lights turning on and off by themselves.

Many of the doors in the pub will open and close on their own. On one occasion, a female employee had asked the ghost to leave when the door she was next to came slamming shut.

2 NORTHWESTERN MINNESOTA

Sturges Park

Location: Buffalo, Wright County, Minnesota
Address: Montrose (Lake) Blvd., Buffalo, MN

Directions: From MN 55 turn west on 2nd Street South to Lake Blvd.

Ghost Lore

Parks frequently offer a retreat from the hectic world of cemented cities. Beautiful Sturges Park is no different. As it quietly rests just off from the main road, it dutifully watches over Buffalo Lake. With picnicking areas, a boat landing, a fishing pier, and boat and bike rentals, the park offers visitors access into the natural world. However, many visitors of the park report that they may be getting more of the supernatural than natural.

- The ghost of a wealthy pioneer man of the 1880s haunts this park.
- The bathroom mirrors are covered with names written in blood.
- Strange glowing balls of lights are reported in the park.

History

1862 – Alfred Eugene Sturges was born. As a young man, Alfred worked as a clerk in the general store.

1882 – Mr. Sturges married Adelaide Covart.

1883 – The Sturgeses built a one-room house on a two-acre piece of land.

1889 – Alfred convinced his dad to purchase a grocery store business.

2 NORTHWESTERN MINNESOTA

1903 – Mr. A.E. Sturges opened his five-acre park along Buffalo Lake to the public.

1916 – The park was sold to the District Conference of the Swedish Free Church.

1935 – Adelaide Sturges died. She was buried in the Lakeview Cemetery.

1956 – Alfred Sturges died at the age of 94. He too was buried in the Lakeview Cemetery.

MINNESOTA ROAD GUIDE TO HAUNTED LOCATIONS

1958 – The park was purchased by the city of Buffalo for $28,000. At the same time, Sturges' daughter, Mrs. Mrya Little, sold some of her land surrounding the park. The city also purchased land around the park owned by W.P. Anderson.

1961 – The park was officially named Sturges Park. The Wright County Retirement Center purchased land for a new facility for $1.

1968 – The new bathrooms were added.

1970 – A new picnic shelter was constructed.

1973 – A skating rink was constructed in the southeast corner of the park.

Investigation

The park is thought to be haunted by A. E. Sturges, the man who first constructed the park.

- Visitors report seeing his ghost wandering around the park near his old home.

- Numerous reports state the place is haunted by a wealthy man of the 1880's. However, Mr. Sturges was not a wealthy man until the 1890's.

- There is writing and marking on the bathroom mirrors, however the writing appears to be done with a marker and not blood.

- We spoke with several residents who had heard of the hauntings of Sturges Park, but did not have any personal experiences.

- During evenings at the park, visitors report seeing strange balls of light floating around. The cause of these lights has not been identified.

MINNESOTA ROAD GUIDE TO HAUNTED LOCATIONS

New York Mills Regional Cultural Center

Location: New York Mills, Otter Tail County, Minnesota
Physical Address: 24 Main Ave N., New York Mills, MN 56567-4318
Mailing Address: P.O. Box 246, New York Mills, MN 56567-0246
Phone: (218) 385-3339
Fax: (218) 385-3366
Website: www.kulcher.org
Email: nymills@kulcher.org

Directions: From Highway 10 turn onto Main Street.

Ghost Lore

If you are looking for one of the coolest small towns in America, then you have to visit New York Mills. Named by several travel writers and *USA Today* as one of America's most funky little towns, New York Mills still has a firm grip on its past as it makes its way into the future. In addition to Lund Boats, the Great American Think Off, the sculpture garden, and the Whistle Stop Inn, the town also has its own haunted building.

- This building was a general store and the previous owner committed suicide in the building.
- Ghostly footsteps have been heard throughout the building.
- Pieces from the gallery move around on their own.

History

1885 – The main building was constructed.

1905 – A one-story building was constructed with a basement to be used as a retail shop.

1900s – The building was used for several businesses.
The building last housed a furniture store before the Regional Arts Project purchased the property.

MINNESOTA ROAD GUIDE TO HAUNTED LOCATIONS

1991 – The city of New York Mills donated $35,000 to the Regional Arts Project. The community came together to save and remodel the old building.

1992 – The New York Mills Regional Cultural Center moved into the vacant building.

Investigation

- We spoke with several staff who believe that the story of the former owner is untrue, although they did confirm that the building was once used as a general store.

- We were unable to find any death of the former owner.

- Staff reported that while they are working alone, they hear someone talking directly to them, yet no one else is in the building.

- A former high school worker reported that she would hear voices while she was working at the center. Whenever she tried to locate these voices, she came up empty handed.

- While working at the center, the staff will hear what sounds like someone walking around on the wood floors, yet when they investigate, they find the place is completely empty.

- Both visitors and staff report feeling a strange presence in the building.

- Staff have encountered other strange noises that cannot be accounted for.

MINNESOTA ROAD GUIDE TO HAUNTED LOCATIONS

Whistle Stop Inn

Location: New York Mills, Otter Tail County, Minnesota
Address: 107 Nowell St. E., New York Mills, MN 56567-4409
Phone: (218) 385-2223
Toll-free: 1-800-328-6315
Website: www.whistlestopbedandbreakfast.com
Email: whistlestop@wcta.net

Directions: From US 10 turn south onto Hwy 67. Take East Centennial Drive to Main Street South. Follow Main Street South for two blocks and turn and east on Nowell Street.

Ghost Lore

If you miss the romance and adventure of the passenger train, or if you have never had the opportunity to experience a night on the train, the Whistle Stop Inn is perfect for you. Conveniently located directed next to a heavily used trail line, this old bed and breakfast will steam power you back to a time when the train dominated the rails. Situated on an acre of flush green land, sprinkled with 150-year old oak trees, the Whistle Stop Inn is complete with three old retired train cars and two rooms in the Victorian home for you to settle into.

- It is said that ghostly footsteps can be heard in the main house.
- Guests have felt a presence in the train cars.

History

The home. Built in 1903 by a Finnish immigrant family, this Victorian era house has retained its charm and grace throughout the years. Once you step inside this home, you will immediately notice the beautiful woodwork and restoration of the home. The home also contains many antiques from the turn of the century.

The train cars. The Imperial Car (Red) was built in 1903, and had 80 seats. The train car ran on the North Coast Limited with runs between the State of Washington and Minnesota. The train car was purchased from the Northern Pacific Company in the 1930's. The train car was first used for a hunting shack. In the 1940's, the train car became a home for a family of four. Continuing its lackluster past, the car was again used for storage until it was purchased for the Whistle Stop Inn and renovated to its past glory.

The Palace Car (Green) was built in 1909, to be used as a club dining car. It was used for this purpose by the Northern Pacific Rail Road Company until the 1960's. The car was then given to a railroad man working at the tie factory in Brainerd as a retirement gift. The man also decided to use the car for storage. The car was used for storage until the roof collapsed. The Whistle Stop Inn spent a year bringing the majestic car back to its original greatness.

The Caboose (Dark Red) enjoys the title of oldest car in the Whistle Stop Inn's collection. Constructed in 1883, the car operated until it became an office for the owner of public storage units in Pelican Lake. The historic caboose was the first car renovated by the Whistle Stop Inn.

2 NORTHWESTERN **MINNESOTA**

Investigation

The Whistle Stop Inn is owned and operated by the super friendly Jann and Roger Lee. They reported that in 1929, the original owner had fallen down the steps of the house and broke her neck. They also stated that the house at one time was a funeral parlor.

A woman staying in the Palace car was leisurely enjoying the whirlpool, when she had an overwhelming scent of men's cologne pass by her.

A couple spent the evening in the second floor room of the main house. In the morning, they reported hearing someone walking past their room several times throughout the night. The owners informed them that no one else was in the house that evening.

Often times Jann will be upstairs when she will hear odd noises coming from the downstairs when no one is there.

Lake Julia Sanitarium

Location: Puposky, Beltrami County, Minnesota
Correction: It is often erroneously called Saint Julia Sanitarium
Address: 308 Great Divide Rd. NW, Puposky, MN 56667-6709

Directions: 12 miles north of Bemidji. Turn Left on 26 which is also Great Divide Rd NW. The building will be at the second driveway on your left.

Ghost Lore

This old abandoned sanatorium is nicely hidden along the rural homes that shield it from the prying eyes of curious visitors. Built with concrete, the building is still in relatively good shape and one can still find original items such as bathtubs and old lighting fixtures. However, most visitors coming to this building are searching for ghosts rather than antiques.

2 NORTHWESTERN MINNESOTA

- Many people falsely believe that the sanatorium is in Bemidji.
- It is said that this building once housed an insane asylum.

History

The building was never an insane asylum; it was always a tuberculosis hospital.

1915 – The site for the sanatorium was chosen under the State Sanatorium Law of 1915. The land was purchased from the Red Lake Railroad at the price of $15 per acre. The original building consisted of two stories and sat on 90 acres of land near the north shore of Lake Julia.

MINNESOTA ROAD GUIDE TO HAUNTED LOCATIONS

1916 – The sanatorium was designed by Minneapolis architects Bund & Dunham. The sanatorium was constructed by W.H. Murphy & Son for the price of $55,000.

1916 – July 10th the first patient, Nels Saltness, arrived at the sanatorium.

1921 – Dr. Laney was hired as the superintendent. Laney purchased another 120 acres and built several buildings on the land including vegetable gardens, greenhouses, and a small electric power plant.

1929 – After having a difficult time finding another superintendent, Mary Ghostley was hired.

MINNESOTA ROAD GUIDE TO HAUNTED LOCATIONS

1953 – When it was discovered that chemotherapy was an effective cure of TB, the sanatorium closed its door.

Investigation

We spoke with several witnesses who claimed to have seen strange floating balls of lights (orbs) travel up the old elevator shaft.

We spoke to two young adults who had seen shadowy figures pass by the broken out windows of the building.

Witnesses report seeing the ghost of a young girl peering at them from the second floor. It should be noted that the women were housed on the second floor, while the men had the first floor.

Visitors report hearing moaning sounds coming from the building, but are unable to find the source of these mysterious sounds.

Note: This is private property. Please, do not trespass.

2 NORTHWESTERN **MINNESOTA**

Redby Store

Location: Redby, Beltrami County, Minnesota
Physical Address: Main St., Redby, MN 56670
Mailing Address: P.O. Box 458, Redby, MN 56670-0458
Phone: (218) 679-3511

Directions: Directions: Right off Highway 1 (the main street through Redby)

Ghost Lore

Many of the mills that once littered Minnesota's small towns are now nothing more than ghost buildings, yet the old mill in Redby may be different, as it is said to actually house a ghost.

- The ghost of an old mill worker carrying his tools still roams the area.

- The ghost can only be seen during the summer after a fresh rain.

History

Many know Redby as the old Chief's Village and was popular for its powwow celebrations up until the 1950's.

1924 – The Redby Saw Mill, also known as the Red Lake Saw Mill, opened.

1984 – Due to financial problems, the plant had to shut down temporarily.

1998 – The sawmill closed for good.

Investigation

Many witnesses actually spot the ghost walking behind the Redby Store. Most think the ghost is a former employee of the mill.

2 NORTHWESTERN MINNESOTA

Apparently it is not true that the spirit only appears after a rain storm. In our investigation we found no correlation between the sightings and weather conditions.

The remains of the town mill are still located behind the store, yet we found no evidence of a man dying there.

The store was formerly known as Westbrook Store.

Many in the town had heard the story of the ghost mill worker, while no one seemed to know the origins of the story, or any specific information as to the identity of the ghost.

We spoke to an employee of the store that recalled seeing the ghost of a man nearly 15 years ago. She spotted the 'man' walking behind the store. It appeared that the ghost was wearing some type of work uniform and was said to be carrying his work tools. As the woman continued to watch the man, he seemed to just disappear.

MINNESOTA ROAD GUIDE TO HAUNTED LOCATIONS

Wendigo

Location: Ross, Roseau County, Minnesota

Directions: From Highway 11 turn north on 89. Search the roads surrounding the town of Ross.

Ghost Lore

For those of you who crave adventure, you will definitely want to investigate this case.

Native Americans believe the Wendigo is a possessed cannibalistic spirit hell bent on finding unwilling human victims to devour or curse. Accounts from the north of Minnesota and regions of Canada state that the creature, or spirit, is nearly 15 feet tall and possesses supernatural powers. Some say it is a former shaman that is cursed to walk the land forever. Regardless of what it is, it has been spotted by residents of northern Minnesota for hundreds of years.

2 NORTHWESTERN MINNESOTA

- If you see the Wendigo, death will soon follow.
- Strange balls of light hover near an old Indian village.

History

In northern Minnesota, near the Canadian border, there was a small Indian village that had many reports of the Wendigo. Actually, many areas in the north had bands of small Indian settlements. Warroad had several Indian camps near the border. The place where most of the sightings took place was at an Indian village near where the small town of Ross stands today. Pioneer explorer Jake Nelson reported the community to be about 40 or so people.

Investigation

Although stories of the Wendigo were told orally for many generations, Nelson was one of the first to write about them. In 1886, Nelson recounts this story of the Wendigo:

> The ghost of the Indian village never appeared right in the village but in the immediate vicinity. The Indians had seen it many times and its appearance always presaged the death of someone at the village. The apparition has been known to the Indians for so long a time that they have no traditions of its first appearance.
>
> The first white persons to see this apparition were Edina T. Nelson and her brother, Jesse Nelson. The former Miss Nelson is now Mrs. S. W. Bennett. The children were going to school and about a mile west they met the apparition in the road. When they came nearly up to it they turned off the road and went around it. On they went to G. Davis's clam shanty which was used as the first school house. Edna and Jesse twice saw this apparition at the same place on the road. They described it as being eight feet tall all dressed in white and having on its forehead a large bright star.

The spirit creature disappeared into the grove of the S.W. Bertilrud farm. Jake Nelson himself reportedly saw the Wendigo. He described it in his writing as "about 15 feet tall, dressed in some material that looked like white lace."

The apparition also appeared to foretell the death of Anna Micninock's mother. Anna Micninock's mother was believed to be over 150 years old and it was said that she was the grandmother of all those in the Indian village. Anna was walking outside the village when she noticed the "Wubagi" moving along the prairie as though it was coming closer to the homes. The apparition was walking out of the muskeg to the west, as though it was stumbling. The apparition then ran for nearly a quarter of a mile where it disappeared into the grove. The old mother died after the sighting and some reports state that Anna died the following day.

Other accounts from the area describe a will-o'-the-wisp haunting the area. In 1886, while building his house near the Indian village Jake Nelson wrote that he noticed a light by a bunch of willows ¼ mile from town. Nelson asked Billy McGillis about the lights and Billy replied, "The light is caused by some gas which rises out of the muskeg." It is said that the light appears every year and the Indians would try to catch it, but they never could. It seemed to float away from them and then come back. Nelson wrote that they thought, "It was too much like playing with the Devil."

We spoke with a local historian who informed us of several sightings of the Wendigo over the last 30 years while residents were driving near Ross. The witnesses describe seeing what appeared to be a Native Indian walking down the road. However, the witnesses reported that the "Indian" was more of a white form that appeared to be wearing a headdress.

Often accounts differ on the gender of the spirit as some witnesses feel it was a male, while others claim that it was a female.

The Skatin' Place

Location: Saint Cloud, Stearns County, Minnesota
Address: 3302 Southway Dr., Saint Cloud, MN 56301-9513
Phone: (320) 252-9768
Reservations: (320) 52-8123
Website: www.skatinplacestcloud.com

Directions: Take County Road 7 south (Clearwater Road), this turns into 33rd Street South. Turn left on Southway Drive and arrive at the Skatin' Place.

Ghost Lore

A lot of strange things happen at a roller rink, from turtle races, and lock-ins, to dance skating, and disco music. However, the Skatin' Place seems to have all of that beat with its very own ghost. As with much of the land that public places now sit on, this area was once said to be a swampy piece of farmland. There is also the story of a young boy dubbed 'Gilbert' who is said to have drowned on the property's swamp years ago.

- Employees report video games turning on and off on their own.
- Strange footsteps are heard coming from the roof.
- Lights turn off and on by themselves.

History

1970s – The Skatin' Place opened.

The property was constructed on farmland.

We were unable to find any evidence of a boy drowning on the old property.

Investigation

We spoke with several employees who informed us that they have all had strange experiences at the rink, yet they were not quite sure if they believed they have a ghost.

Employees report that the rink's video games will inexplicably turn on and off by themselves.

One employee closed up on a Friday night and made sure that all the lights were turned off, yet when she came in the next morning to open the rink, the lights had been mysteriously turned on.

A female employee was working up in the front of the rink making pizzas for the day, when she heard the air hockey puck handles start moving on their own even though the machine was not on.

The owner often hears the sound of footsteps on top of the building while no one is present.

A young female customer came up to staff and reported that she had just seen a scary face in the vent while she was skating. When staff went to investigate, they found no source of the face.

An employee stated that while no music was in the CD players, she heard the Ghostbusters song being played over the speakers.

2 NORTHWESTERN MINNESOTA

Two employees were working when they heard what sounded like the exit door in the laser tag room being slammed shut. When they quickly investigated, they found no one near the door.

One former employee would often report hearing weird noises like something crackling, yet she could never find the cause.

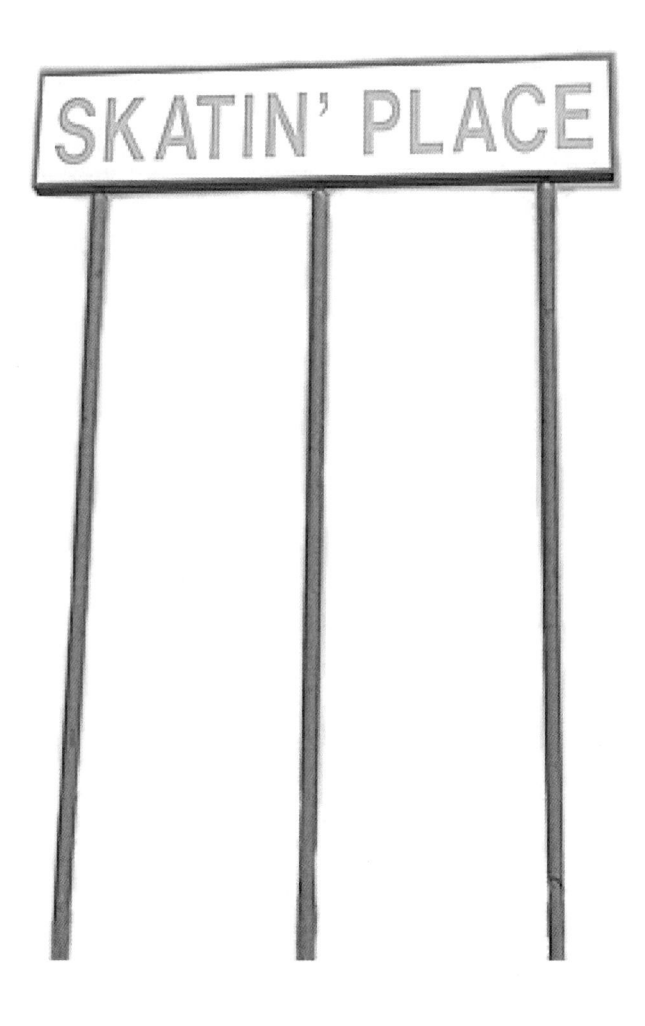

Oakland Cemetery

Location: Sauk Centre, Stearns County, Minnesota
Address: 393rd Ave, Sauk Centre, MN 56378-8347

Directions: Take Sinclair Lewis Ave (17) to the east. Turn south (right) on 185. Take the curve (393rd Ave.) to the right down the dirt road and the cemetery will be on your left.

Ghost Lore

Cemeteries are often considered to be a hotbed of paranormal activity and the secluded Oakdale Cemetery is no different. Oakdale Cemetery rests on an old country dirt road on the outside of the tourist friendly town of Sauk Centre. This moderate sized cemetery gives visitors a creepy feel as they realize the seclusion of the cemetery. Filled with a mixture of old and new gravesites, this cemetery is secured by a front fence complete with a squeaky gate.

2 NORTHWESTERN MINNESOTA

- A gravestone in the cemetery will glow late at night.
- Ghosts of young children haunt this graveyard.

Investigation

The gravestone in question is a rather normal looking gravestone with the name BOSS etched on it. According to the *Sauk Centre Herald,* the story of the glowing stone has been around for many years. The *Herald* reported that retired police officer Bud Nordine has been going out to the cemetery to show people the glowing stone for years. According to the report, Bud believes that the stone is possibly reflecting light from the town.

The stone does rest on a slightly elevated mound giving to the theory that light from the nearby town of Sauk Centre shines onto the stone and makes it glow. It should also be noted that there is a cluster of trees and brush blocking the gravestone's direct light path to the town.

Looking at the gravestones beneath the headstone reveals that two infants are buried at the location. One infant named Babe was born and died in 1886, and the other infant Arthur was born and died in 1881. These two untimely deaths may contribute to the stories surrounding the strange anomalies that haunt the gravestone.

We spoke with a witness who had been out to the cemetery and on several occasions had seen the gravestone glowing. The man was certain that he was not seeing the reflection of city lights.

The Palmer House Hotel

Location: Sauk Centre, Stearns County, Minnesota
Address: The Palmer House Hotel, 500 Sinclair Lewis Ave., Sauk Centre, MN 56378-1246
Phone: (320) 351-9100
Website: www.thepalmerhousehotel.com

Directions: Follow Main Street off of Highway 71 to Sinclair Lewis Avenue.

Ghost Lore

- A young boy died while staying at the hotel and he can be seen and heard bouncing his ball down the hallways.

- A man haunts many of the rooms of the hotel and is believed to throw glasses in the bar.

- Mysterious knocks have been heard from several of the rooms in the hotel.

MINNESOTA ROAD GUIDE TO HAUNTED LOCATIONS

- The hotel is haunted by Sinclair Lewis.
- There are bodies and bones buried beneath the hotel in the basement.

History

On the corner of Sinclair Lewis Avenue and the original Main Street rests the historic Palmer House. The original hotel, The Sauk Center House as it was known to locals, was constructed in 1863 by Warren Adley. In 1867, the property was purchased by E.P. Barnum. During this time both the staff and the locals referred to the hotel as the Minnesota House. In 1868, the new owner, John Apfeld, changed the name of the building to the Apfeld House. On June 26th, 1900 the hotel burned to the ground. According to all newspaper accounts, the fire was intentional and the town seemed relieved that the hotel was gone, as it was considered a sore on the community by attracting devious characters. When the city council refused to offer the funds to construct a new hotel, the Sauk Centre Herald stepped forward with an offer of $5,000 to anyone who would build a new hotel.

In 1901, the property was purchased by R.L. Palmer. Mr. Palmer constructed a three-story hotel he named the Palmer House. The hotel originally contained 38 cozy rooms with the guests sharing a communal bathroom at the end of the hall. The concept of having electricity in a hotel was so new, that a special contractor from Minneapolis was brought in to do the work. On October 17th, 1901, the majestic Palmer House opened its doors to the welcoming public.

Sauk Centre proudly boasts itself as the boyhood home of the famous American writer, Sinclair Lewis. In 1902, shortly after the opening of Palmer House, Sinclair Lewis was employed as a bellhop and night clerk. It is rumored that Sinclair was fired from the Palmer House because he spent too much of his time writing and not enough time working. In 1908, the Palmer House was leased out to A.W. Austin. This trend was continued until 1916, when Art DeBeau purchased the hotel from Mr. Palmer.

In 1921, the hotel was sold once again to a George A. Tanner. Over the next few years the hotel switched hands often. Each new owner would make additions and improvements as their finances permitted.

Throughout the years, the Palmer Hotel faded in its glory and became more dilapidated with each passing year. However, in 1974, two business partners purchased the hotel with the intent to restore it to its original beauty. The partners, Al Tingley and Dick Schwartz, had the grand idea to once again restore the Palmer Hotel. In addition to the numerous renovations and upkeep, Al had time to write a book of stories from the Palmer House titled Corner on Main Street.

After Al and Dick, the Palmer House again traded hands quite a few times over years. Today the beautiful hotel is owned and operated by the super friendly and inviting Kelley Freese and her husband. Even though the Palmer Hotel has come a long way, now having 20 gorgeous rooms with four magnificent whirlpool suites, it still hasn't forgotten its cozy small town feel that will leave you craving just one more night.

Investigation

We have been able to track reports of the Palmer Hotel being haunted back many years to when Al Tingley owned the hotel. Although we are certain that the hotel was said to be haunted for much longer, unfortunately no written history of it exists today. With so many stories and witnesses, it was difficult to report them all.

We were also unable to determine whether bodies are buried under the hotel. However, the current owner Kelley did discover some bones in the dirt floor section of the basement, yet when she wanted to have them analyzed, they could not be found.
We were unable to verify whether a little boy actually died in the

hotel. However former owner Al Tingley writes in his book, Corner on Main Street, that he heard the Quinns talking about a ghost back in the 50's. In addition to the ghost stories, Al also had heard that someone had committed suicide upstairs and another man supposedly hanged himself in the Palmer Hotel bar by jumping off the pool table. We were also unable to verify this information; however we do believe that given the history of the hotel, as with other similar historic places, many deaths and tragic events took place.

We spoke with Virgil, a former resident of the Hotel, who rented a room from 1974-1987. Virgil informed us that he often heard the stories of the hotel being haunted and actually heard several knocks on his door, yet could never find anyone there.

The current owner Kelley told us of many nights in which both she and the night clerk would hear what sounded like a boy bouncing a ball down the hall and then chasing after it. Kelley also informed us that quite often the children of guests will report seeing a "young boy" perched on the steps leading up to the second floor. One of the old owners claims to have seen the boy sitting on the staircase and when she asked him what he wanted, he disappeared. One guest wrote in the Hotel's ghost report book that the little boy "has green eyes and dirty blonde hair and his little ball is blue."

Several guests have reported that although everything in the hotel was above their expectations, someone had let their kid run through the hallways all night long. The owner was very hesitant to tell them that on those nights, no children were staying at the hotel. Another guest complained to the owner that whoever was staying in the room above them was continually moving the furniture around. The owner escorted the guest up to the empty room to discover that no furniture had moved. Occasionally a couple of guests, unaware of the hotel's possible haunting, will get spooked out of their rooms and have to leave the hotel for unknown reasons.

Kelley also told us of weird electrical disturbances, including bedroom lights flickering and TVs turning on and off on their own. It should be noted that all the electrical wiring had just been gutted and redone and we found no electrical leaks in the rooms.

The bar has also experienced a fair share of odd activity. A man walked into the bar and ordered a drink and informed the bartender that he would take it upstairs, however upon investigation the staff found that there was no man staying upstairs. Bartenders also told us that glasses that are stored on hanging hooks under the bar, have come flying off the hooks landing and breaking clear across the room. The kitchen staff reported that glasses fly out of storage and break, with no apparent cause. One restaurant employee would routinely setup the tables at night only to come in the next morning and find the silverware had been rearranged. It happened so often that the employee finally decided to set the table right before breakfast.

A newlywed couple were on their honeymoon staying in room 17

(the room we stayed in) when the wife awoke to see the ghost of a tall slender man standing at the edge of the bed looking at her. The woman told us that the man looked as though he was from the 1920s or 1930s. The same couple reported that whenever they left the room and came back, someone or something had turned the heat all the way up. Room 17 is also where a man spending a summer night awoke to find this room so cold that he could see his own breath, even though the air conditioner was not on.

Room 11 is often the site of many reports. One man staying in room 11 was not able to sleep with his legs inside the covers so he placed them over the covers and went back to sleep. He awoke in the middle of the night with the sensation of someone stroking his legs, although no one was visible. Room 11 is also said to be forever cold, as the room needs to be heated while other rooms are using the air conditioner. Many guests report a heavy feeling while staying in this room, and several guests have stated that the energy is originating from the sink.

2 NORTHWESTERN MINNESOTA

Dead Man's Trail

Location: Thief River Falls, Pennington County, Minnesota
Address: Along the Thief River

Directions: There is a seven-mile stretch of official trail along the Thief River. There are many access points to the trail. One main entrance point is next to Hugo's Grocery.

Ghost Lore

When your town is named Thief River Falls, people may expect odd things to take place. This may be an understatement, as we do not know if the town is home to any thieves, but it certainly is home to many haunted stories.

- Native American spirits have been spotted along the trail.

- A mysterious cave along the river was boarded up for unknown reasons.

- Cold chills have been felt along the trail.

History

1730s – Many Native American tribes traveled through northern Minnesota.

1770 – The Chippewa were the main tribe in the Thief River Falls area.

1863 – A treaty between the tribes and the US Government opened up a large area of land for homesteaders.

1880 – The land was permanently settled by white pioneers.

1904 – The final government land sale was held. It closed several days later after the sale of 93,000 acres.

2 NORTHWESTERN **MINNESOTA**

Investigation

There are several tales as to the origin of the town's name. One of the more mundane explanations of the town name is that it is nothing more than a mistranslation of the town's original Indian name.

Another legend of the name states that a ferocious Sioux warrior who was wanted on charges of murder commonly used the Thief River as a hide out for his many robbing expeditions.

Researcher Key Teeters Asp wrote about the third and most elaborate legend that revolves around a young Indian maiden who was desperately trying to escape her pursuers. The young woman set down her crying boy near the river with the intentions of retrieving him once she had eluded those chasing her. However, the baby boy was accidentally swept away in the river and his body tumbled over the waterfall to the rocks below. The young maiden escaped her pursuers only to find her dead child lying on the rocks. She then said that the river had stolen her tribe's future chief. For this great loss, she cursed the river as Thief River. Even today, many years later, those who approach the river can still see and hear the young maiden weeping for her lost child.

Several visitors to the trail report seeing the ghost of this young maiden who seems to be searching for her child.

We also spoke with a life long resident of Thief River Falls who had never heard of the ghost stories or of the trail being called "Dead Man's Trail."

There are over seven miles of walking trail on the Thief River Walkway. There are many more miles of unofficial trails that run alongside the river. We were unable to find any boarded up cave, yet we concede that there may be many caves sprinkled along the river.

SOUTHEASTERN MINNESOTA

Vang Lutheran Church

Location: Dennison, Goodhue County, Minnesota
Location Address: 2060 County 49 Blvd., Dennison, MN 55018-7624
Mailing Address: P.O. Box 117, Dennison, MN 55018-0117
Phone: (507) 645-6042
Email: dennvang@clear.lakes.com

Directions: Take County Highway 9 to 20th Ave. Turn south (only option) on 20th Avenue. Take 20th Avenue for 2.5 miles until you reach County Blvd 49. The church is on the corner of 20th Avenue and 49 Blvd 49.

Ghost Lore

Hidden out in the country among wheat and cornfield stands the Vang Lutheran Church. The church serves as a living history of the congregation's origins. However, the old church may very well also serve as a history of its dead.

3 SOUTHEASTERN MINNESOTA

- Strange voices have been heard throughout the church.
- The congregation was said to have captured a photo of an apparition moving through the church in the 1930's.

History

1862 – The congregation comprised of mostly Norwegians began with the fallout of the Holden Parish.

1863 – The church was designed by the nation's first deaf architect, Olof Hanson. The congregation named the new church "'Vang," which is the Norwegian word for lawn and the name of the church back in Norway. The church was constructed next to the Vang cemetery.

1868 – The Vang Church was dedicated.

1884 – A parsonage was constructed across the street from the church.

1894-1895 – The original church was razed.

1896 – The new Vang Church was constructed at its current location 1 mile north of the cemetery.

Investigation

Many websites have this church wrongly located in Northfield instead of Dennison.

We spoke with the current pastor of the church who informed us that he had heard of the stories, yet had never seen the photo of the apparition. We were also unable to find the photo of the apparition.

We also spoke with several residents of the nearby area who had heard of the church being haunted, yet had no personal experiences.

3 SOUTHEASTERN MINNESOTA

With an average of 75 people attending the church each Sunday, the small congregation has reported seeing strange apparitions throughout the old building.

A witness informed us that while out at the church one evening, he and his friends noticed strange lights in church although no one appeared to be in the church.

MINNESOTA ROAD GUIDE TO HAUNTED LOCATIONS

LeDuc Mansion

Location: Hastings, Dakota County, Minnesota
Address: 1629 Vermillion St., Hastings, MN 55033-3139

Ghost Lore

This 15-room Gothic Revival mansion was constructed using a design by the famous architect Andrew Jackson Downing, and is one of the best-preserved examples of his work in the world. When you take the wonderful tour of the historic LeDuc Mansion, you are told numerous times that General LeDuc was a restless man. Maybe even after death, his spirit continues to be restless.

- There are mysterious tunnels running under the mansion.
- A former resident of the house still haunts the place.
- The LeDucs practiced spiritualism and continue to haunt their former home.

History

1853 – William LeDuc moved to Hastings from Saint Paul.

1862 – Construction for the majestic LeDuc home began. The LeDucs felt that they would have to pay around $2,000 for the home, and they feared estimates of $5,000. After several trying years, the home was finally completed in 1865, at a whopping cost of over $30,000.

1877 – The house was temporary shut down while LeDuc served as the first Secretary of Agriculture in Washington.

1890s – The LeDuc women started Hastings Needlework Company to supplement the family's falling income.

1917 – General LeDuc died at the age of 94.

1941 – The LeDucs were about to lose the house due to the depression when a friend of the family, Carroll Simmons, decided to purchase the house.

1958 – Mr. Simmons donated the home to the Minnesota Historical Society. He was the first person in Minnesota to donate a home to a historical society. However, one condition of the sale was that Mr. Simmons would be allowed to continue to operate his antique business in the home for as long as he wished.

1985 – Carroll Simmons closed his antique shop and the house sat empty for 20 years.

2005 – In May, after numerous renovations, the mansion opened for tours.

Investigation

There are no tunnels that run directly under the mansion. However, the city of Hastings is filled with tunnels leading all over the small town.

Both General LeDuc and his daughter Alice were heavily into spiritualism. This was common for many families throughout the US during the turn of the 1900s.

We spoke with several residents who informed us that they had heard stories of the mansion being haunted dating back to the 1950s.

One woman stated that she remembered visiting the home when Mr. Simmons owned it, and the stories of the house being haunted were circulating at that time.

When Mr. Simmons owned the place, many paperboys were scared to deliver the daily paper to his home. They thought the place was too spooky, and they had heard that it was haunted by several ghosts.

One volunteer told us stories of the doors in the mansion mysteriously opening and slamming shut on their own.

We spoke with the director of the museum who has not had a personal experience at the mansion. She did state that if there are ghosts in the mansion, they are welcoming ghosts. She also stated that the home could be haunted by several different ghosts for various reasons including:

> **Alice.** She was the history buff of the family, and was also heavily into spiritualism.
>
> **William.** He was also interested in the family history, and really loved his home.
>
> **Mr. Simmons.** He owned the place for many years and always kept it dark and spooky.

3 SOUTHEASTERN **MINNESOTA**

Phantom of the Mantorville Opera House

Location: Mantorville, Dodge County, Minnesota
Mailing Address: Mantorville Theatre Company, PO Box 194, Mantorville, MN 55955-0194
Reservations: (507) 635-5420
Email: mantorvilletheatre@yahoo.com
Website: www.mantorvillain.com

Directions: Mantorville is located about 75 miles south of the Twin Cities and 15 miles west of Rochester on Minnesota Highway 57. Turn west on 5th St. The Opera house is on the left side.

Ghost Lore

- The historic theatre has spirits that like to do their performing backstage.

3 SOUTHEASTERN MINNESOTA

- An actress was backstage in the dressing room putting on her costume when a woman walked in wearing the same outfit. The mysterious woman claimed she had played the same role in the same play many years prior, then she vanished from the room. Other actors have had similar experiences of seeing ghosts wearing the same costumes they were.

- Actors have seen shadowy figures up in the rafters.

- People report seeing a ghostly woman dressed in black with a forlorn expression on her face.

History

1918 – The Mantorville Opera House was built on the old foundation of a general store after the business district was destroyed by fire. Many traveling shows performed there. Later it was used as the City Hall and Civic Center.

Today the Mantorville Theatre Company owns it and presents live melodramas from June through August.

MINNESOTA ROAD GUIDE TO HAUNTED LOCATIONS

Investigation

We spoke with several of the people involved with the Mantorville Theatre Company, and all of them insist that something strange is going on in this old theatre. There is apparently a female entity that frequently makes herself known. She is such a regular visitor that people decided she needed a name, so they have dubbed her "Ellen." People frequently have the feeling of being watched, of not being alone, and of having the hair on the back of their neck stand up. One person was sitting alone in the theatre and distinctly heard a woman clear her throat three times. Nobody was there.

Many people report what they refer to as a ghostly game of "light tag." This frequently happens when the last person to leave the theatre at night shuts off the lights and locks the doors, only to discover that one of the upstairs lights have been turned back on. They return to the building, shut off the lights again, and exit only to find the lights have once again been turned on. There have been times when the local police are patrolling the area late at night and find the theatre lights on, but the building is empty. Even after having electricians inspect the wiring, they have not found a rational explanation for this phenomenon.

MINNESOTA ROAD GUIDE TO HAUNTED LOCATIONS

Cheryl Frarck, one of the directors, reported that the ghosts also like to play games with their props. Frarck was playing a character who wore granny-style eyeglasses, and after each performance she would consistently leave them in the pocket of the apron that was part of her costume. One day they were missing from the pocket, but the next day she found two pair in there.

During another performance the actors had a tray of cups, and one of them turned the cups right-side up and poured water into each of them, and they all proceeded to drink. To everybody's surprise, one of the actors started gagging and choking and spitting. Upon inspection, they found that the mug of water that had just been poured for her was now filled with dry sawdust.

Four cast members were in the green room, and they could distinctly hear the sound of a man wearing boots walking down the upstairs hallway towards the stairs. Without hesitation, the frightened thespians ran out of the building.

MINNESOTA ROAD GUIDE TO HAUNTED LOCATIONS

The Kahler Grand Hotel

Location: Rochester, Olmsted County, Minnesota
Address: 20 2nd Ave. SW, Rochester, MN 55902-3027
Phone: (507) 280-6200
Toll-free: 1-800-533-1655
Fax: (507) 285-2701
Website: www.kahler.com
Email: KahlerInfo@sunstonehotels.com

Ghost Lore

The ghost of a missing woman rides the elevators of the hotel.

History

1921 – The Kahler Grand Hotel, located in the heart of downtown Rochester, was built and later renovated in 1994. Because it is connected to the Mayo Clinic complex, many of the visiting patients stay there.

3 SOUTHEASTERN **MINNESOTA**

1977 – Brach candy heiress Helen Voorhees Brach, 65, visited the Mayo Clinic in Rochester for a checkup. The doctors found her to be in good health, she paid her bill, checked out of her room at the Kahler Grand Hotel, made some purchases at a gift shop, and then left. This was the last time that anybody had seen her.

1984 – Brach was declared to be legally dead.

1988 – Criminal investigator Catherine Denenberg traveled to New Jersey to consult the famed psychic detective Dorothy Allison. Allison told her Brach met her death by fire or cremation.

1991 – Denenberg made a second visit to Allison. This time the psychic tells her that Brach's body was taken to Inland Steel and incinerated. Denenberg took careful notes of the things Allison described and later presented them to the state's attorney, Jack O'Malley, who, unfortunately, refused to allow investigators to pursue leads obtained from a psychic. The information from Allison was never made public.

2005 – An individual named Joe Plemmons came forward and confessed to his involvement in the murder of Helen Brach. According to Plemmons, he and ten others beat and shot her to death, then incinerated her body at the Inland Steel Mill near Gary, Indiana--just as Dorothy Allison had said.

Catherine Denenberg still has the handwritten notes she took in her interview with Dorothy Allison. The paper is yellowed with age, but it still verifies the accuracy of the psychic's information.

Investigation

When Helen Brach first disappeared, photos of her were displayed in newspapers and on television, and a lot of people were keeping an eye out for her. Curiously, most of the sightings that were reported centered around the Kahler Hotel and specifically the elevators.

We spoke with several of the employees at the hotel who were convinced that it is haunted. Still to this day, people report seeing Brach riding the elevators and vanishing before their eyes.

3 SOUTHEASTERN **MINNESOTA**

Anderson House

Location: Wabasha, Wabasha County, Minnesota
Official Name: Historic Anderson House
Address: 333 Main St. W., Wabasha, MN 55981-1218
Phone: (651) 565-2500
Fax: (651) 565-2600
Website: www.historicandersonhouse.com

Directions: From Hwy 39/51 go east on Hwy 73. The immediate first left turn is 5th Ave. Follow this road around the corner until you see the cemetery on the right.

Ghost Lore

Anchoring the main street of Wabasha along the beautiful Mississippi River is the Historic Anderson House. Perched overlooking the majestic river, the Anderson House contains 22 sleeping rooms and an in-house restaurant. Whether you are staying in a cozy single room or one of the beautiful whirlpool suites, you will

MINNESOTA ROAD GUIDE TO HAUNTED LOCATIONS

feel as though you have been transported back through time to when life moved at a slower pace.

Even though the Anderson House is known for its historic charm and hospitality, it is even better known for the beautiful cats that you can request to sleep in your room. The tradition of cats staying with guests is said to have started with a man who often stayed at the hotel on his many visits to the Mayo Clinic. The man talked so much about how he missed sleeping with his cat, that the owner loaned him one of her cats to sleep with. The lending of cats has been a tradition ever since.

- The house is haunted by a woman who took her own life with a knife and now pays visits to unsuspecting guests.

- A ghostly man dressed with a top hat lurks the halls of the house.

- The house cats are terrified of certain rooms and cower under the bed.

- Televisions and their remotes often short out or just stop working.

- The radio station in the kitchen would often change stations by itself.

History

1856 – Blois Hurd constructed a two-story hotel. Blois served as the Sheriff of the county for many years. Blois passed away on November 3, 1896, and his remains are buried in the Riverview Cemetery.

1887 – Zilba (Z. C.) Goss renovated the old Hurd House by adding a third floor and western wing. Mr. Goss was a native of Vermont and relocated to Wabasha in the fifties when his father, John Goss, moved to a farmstead in the Township of Highland. At 18, Goss enlisted in Company G of the Third Minnesota Volunteer Infantry. Trained as a carpenter and builder, Goss had a vision of a hotel that would be equipped with all the modern accommodations of a big city hotel. He fulfilled this vision with the Hurd House. The new Hurd House was a three-story solid brick structure containing 45 lavish rooms complete with first class furnishings. The hotel contained modern bathrooms, electric service bells, and electric lights. The cost of the hotel was over $10,000.

1909 – The Hurd House was purchased by William H. Anderson and his wife Ida. Mr. Anderson was born in New York where he completed grammar school and came to Minnesota in 1866. He worked a farm near his brother, A.J. Anderson, in Hammond. William also worked as a stock buyer at Zumbro for over six years.

3 SOUTHEASTERN MINNESOTA

In 1896, Anderson migrated to Mazeppa, purchased the Mongan House, and renamed it the Anderson House. In 1909, Anderson moved from Mazeppa to Wabasha to purchase his new Anderson House.

1920 – J. H. McCaffrey and his wife Verna purchased the Anderson Hotel from her father, William Anderson. The couple also made many changes to the hotel by redecorating the dining room, bathrooms, kitchen, and many of the living apartments.

1938 – Ida Anderson passed away.

1939 – Mr. McCaffrey passed away, leaving his wife Verna to run the hotel. Mrs. McCaffrey summoned the aid of her sister, Mrs. Belle Anderson Ebner, to assist with running the hotel.

1945 – The hotel was managed by Verna's daughter, Jean Hemsey.

1964 – The hotel was sold to Mr. William Shepherd

1974 – John Hall, son of Jean Hemsey, managed the hotel. This marked the return of the hotel to an Anderson.

2002 – Patrick Wilson owned the hotel.

2004 – Mike and Teresa Smith purchased the hotel.

Investigation

The new owners were told by previous owners that in 1859, a woman named Sarah lived in the house with her husband, who was a fisherman. One day, the husband set out on the river and he never returned. Sarah was so distraught and heartbroken over the loss of her husband, that she killed herself with a knife near what is now room 25.

We were unable to find any story of a "Sarah" committing suicide at the house.

3 SOUTHEASTERN MINNESOTA

We spoke with the owner who informed us that she feels that there are many spirits at the house. She also feels that these spirits are at peace.

A woman staying in room 32 was sleeping when she was woken by something saying her name and touching her shoulder. However, when she opened her eyes, no one was there. The woman was extremely confused because her view of the room was in black and white.

A young girl staying at the house with her family saw two ghosts walking on the staircase that connects the second floor with the third floor. The girl stated that one of the ghosts was a man who appeared to be wearing an old top hat.

MINNESOTA ROAD GUIDE TO HAUNTED LOCATIONS

A woman staying in room 10 reported that the hotel cat that was accompanying her kept chasing after something unseen and repeatedly jumped at the wall as though something was there.

When a guest was staying in room two, they witnessed a lamp and a clock fly off the table for no apparent reason, while a cup of coffee on the table remained untouched.

The owners report that many of the newer TVs will stop working for no apparent reason. The remotes to these TVs will also stop working, even with new batteries.

In 2005, several psychics stayed at the home and reported that many of the rooms were haunted by spirits. It was in room 25 that the psychics believed they saw two shadowy figures pass between the walls.

3 SOUTHEASTERN MINNESOTA

Pieces of the Past

Location: Winona, Winona County, Minnesota
Address: 79 E. 2nd St., Winona, MN 55987-3443
Phone: (507) 452-3722
Website: www.piecesofthepast-winona.com
Email: country2@hbci.com

Directions: From Highway 43 turn east on East Second Street

Ghost Lore

This old Second Street building was located near the old train station, making it a popular spot for travelers and locals alike. The building also attracted some of the area's more undesirable characters. The building was once a roaring hotel, saloon, and brothel. It is said that one of the ladies of the night was shot and killed on the main staircase. Her ghost is often seen and heard throughout the building.

History

Pre-1884 – History unknown.

1884 – The building was standing on what was known as the Ely Block.

1888 – Was the Mississippi House—a hotel and brothel with many working ladies.

1900 – Henry Wehrenberg owned the building that was used for AA Artz beds (hotel).

1905 – Winona Candy Company occupied the building; selling cigars, nuts, and chocolates.

1921 – Louis Miller and Son Junk Hides and Furs also occupied some of the space with the candy store. They also sold metals and rubber rags.

1931 – Winona Radiator and Sheet Metal Works rented space in the building.

1933 – Cal's Auto Body Service moved in.

1941 – The Sunrise Café takes over the building. The cafe was operated by Henry Zellman selling beer, wine, liquors, and lunches.

1988 – The building sat unoccupied.

1990s – Several bars occupied the building including Bangers, Jack's Bar, and Fiten's Bar.

2000 – Duane and Cheri Peterson opened Pieces of the Past.

Investigation

We were unable to find any story of a woman being killed in the building.

Gina Teel writes in her book, *Ghost Stories of Minnesota*, that many former bartenders lived in the apartments directly above the bar and often reported hearing extremely loud noises downstairs when the bar was empty. When the bartenders went to investigate, they came up empty handed. The employees also stated that on many occasions, the ghost appeared in the apartment rooms above the bar.

The current owner informed us that items would periodically fly off the shelf for no reason. This happens mostly to the merchandise that is located on the old dance floor. The staff is unable to find any cause for this anomaly, and often attribute it to the ghost of the store.

On Halloween, the owner had the store decorated with toy ghouls that would shake and scream when someone passed in front of them. These ghouls were positioned to go off when someone entered the store. The door was also rigged with chimes that would ring when the front door was opened or closed. While working in the back room, the owner heard the toy ghouls go off, yet the chimes were silent. This occurred several times and on each occasion, the front door remained locked.

The owner was in the back room closing up, when he started to walk back upstairs, the air got eerily cold and the owner flippantly said "good night" to the ghosts, only to hear the chimes of the front door ring. When he got to the front door, he was surprised to find that it had not been moved and was still locked.

One of the staff members was working at the store when she felt something touch her on the shoulder. Thinking it was a co-worker or customer she turned around to see who it was. What she found was that no one was there.

When in the store, employees often report running into unexplainable cold spots. Although the staff have tried to locate the source of the cold spots, they have been unable to do so.

Winona Family YMCA

Location: Winona, Winona County, Minnesota
Address: 207 Winona St., Winona, MN 55987-3165
Phone: (507) 454-1520
Website: www.winonafamilyymca.com

Directions: From Highway 43 turn south on Winona Street.

Ghost Lore

The YMCA is one of Winona's oldest and most cherished organizations. The YMCA is set up to provide recreation activities to the general public including swimming, yoga, camping, personal trainers, and much more. However, while most people go to the YMCA for a quick workout, others travel to the Y to see the ghost.

- A former janitor is haunting the building.
- Doors mysteriously open and close on their own.

MINNESOTA ROAD GUIDE TO HAUNTED LOCATIONS

History

1885 – Eleven businessmen met at the home of Rudolph McBurnie to discuss the possibility of a YMCA in Winona.

1886-1889 – First meeting of the Winona YMCA was held in the parlor of the Presbyterian Church.

1889-1895 – The YMCA was located in the Stevens building.

1900 – The first permanent YMCA is located on Fifth and Main Street.

1906-1907 – The town of Winona dedicated the official YMCA building. At a cost of $65,000, the YMCA was complete with a swimming pool, banquet room, and a barbershop.

1915 – The YMCA expanded with a gymnasium.

1916-1920 – The YMCA started to deteriorate.

1946 – A fire caused by the coal stoker destroyed the original YMCA. No one was killed in the fire.

1946 – Operating out of several satellite spots, the YMCA planned its rebuilding.

1951 – The new facility opened at its current location.

1969 – The YMCA expanded with a second gym.

1985 – The name was officially changed to the Winona Family YMCA.

Currently the YMCA is still used for recreation.

Investigation

We spoke with the executive director who informed us that although he had heard of the ghost stories, he had never had a personal experience. The director also stated that the YMCA has had many staff and renters throughout the years, and it is possible that several who passed away were attached to the YMCA.

One employee reported hearing strange noises while working at the Y, but had always attributed it to the building being old.

Staff have reported the sighting of a man who was believed to be a former janitor of the organization.

SOUTHWESTERN MINNESOTA

MINNESOTA ROAD GUIDE TO HAUNTED LOCATIONS

The Ghost of the Clock Tower

Location: Albert Lea, Freeborn County, Minnesota
Address: Freeborn County Courthouse, 411 S. Broadway,
P.O. Box 1147, Albert Lea, MN 56007-1147
Phone: (507) 377-5192
Fax: (507) 377-5196

Ghost Lore

The courthouse is haunted by the ghost of an unidentified man who hanged himself in the clock tower many years ago.

History

In 1938, an unknown man took his life in the tallest and most remote part of the courthouse.

His body was discovered about 8:00 am on July 5, 1938, when custodian Bill Groetke went up to the tower to reset the clock. When Groetke pushed open the trap door to reach the tower, he turned pale upon seeing the wide-open mouth of a man with bulging eyes staring down at him. He quickly retreated to get the sheriff and coroner, and they came to examine the badly decomposing body of a man hanging from the rafter in the topmost section of the courthouse tower.

The unknown man had apparently carried a ladder up into the tower so he could tie a rope to the rafters. Authorities had found that he had carefully cut out all the labels and laundry marks from his

The Freeborn County Courthouse when the clock tower was still intact. The tower and turrets were removed in 1953. *Photo courtesy of The Freeborn County Historical Society.*

clothing. The only thing found in his pockets was the case for his eyeglasses, and he had even removed the brand name from the case.

He was middle-aged and had reddish-brown hair. The coroner estimated that his body had been in the tower for several weeks. His body was placed in a box, and workers had to use a block and tackle arrangement to lower his body from the tower to the ground. Hundreds of spectators gathered to watch the two-hour operation.

On July 6, the body was positively identified as that of a saxophone player known as George "Red" Russell. This musician had played with the Ray Keyes Orchestra in Albert Lea for about ten weeks until he disappeared. His parents, who lived in North Carolina, were notified by telegram, and they authorized his temporary burial.

Shortly after his burial, "Red" turned up in Waterloo, Iowa playing with another orchestra. The authorities admitted their mistake.

On July 8, authorities again announced that they had identified the unknown man. The second "Red" was a former courthouse employee who had assisted the custodian with the clock tower maintenance. This man, originally from Fairmont, had attempted suicide on two prior occasions. He had served time in prison for forgery, and had been listed as missing for several weeks. The police were confident that they had correctly identified John Doe until his fingerprints were found to not match the prints on file at the state prison. This missing Fairmont man was later found alive and well in another part of the country.

Over the years, the police have had a few tips and clues, but they have always been false leads. To this day, the identity of the hanged man remains to be one of the greatest mysteries in the history of Albert Lea.

Investigation

Many employees and visitors at the courthouse have reported ghostly phenomena.

- Solid, three-inch thick wooden doors will slam on their own.
- People hear the sounds of footsteps, creaking stairs, and other strange noises.
- Apparitions of the unidentified man have been seen wandering the hallways.

Le Sueur County Historical Society Museum

Location: Elysian, Le Sueur County, Minnesota
Address: 301 2nd St. N.E., Elysian, MN 56028-2008
Phone: (507) 267-4620
Website: www.frontiernet.net/~lchsmuseum

Directions: While on Highway 60, turn north on 2nd Street. Take 2nd Street three blocks to the corner of 2nd Street and Frank Street.

Ghost Lore

Many researchers speculate that spirits not only attach themselves to locations, but many attach themselves to specific items. If this is the case, then the Le Sueur County Museum may have over 24,000 ghosts. The first thing you notice when visiting this county museum is the sheer number of historical pieces contained within the old schoolhouse. With everything from archeological finds to re-creations of 1900s bedrooms, this museum will have something for even the fussiest history buff.

For the last eight years, the museum has been run by Nancy Burhop. Serving as the museum's director, Nancy casts a welcoming feel over the museum. Nancy takes a refreshingly down to earth approach as she calmly states that she feels the place is definitely haunted.

- Playful ghosts haunt the old schoolhouse.
- Odd noises can be heard throughout the museum.
- Employees report being touched by unseen visitors.
- Many psychics have visited the museum and concluded that the museum has many visitors not signed in on the guest book.

MINNESOTA ROAD GUIDE TO HAUNTED LOCATIONS

History

The three-floored building was constructed as the Elysian Public School in 1895. Several grades were separated into various rooms throughout the building. However, not one person graduated from this school, as all the students had to finish their education through a nearby school.

1963 – The building was no longer used as a school.

The building sat empty for two years.

1965 – The historical society purchased the building for $14.50. The story is that while at a city meeting, tearing down the old schoolhouse was discussed when the historical society stated that they could use it for a museum. One member of the audience was so anxious to get on with the meeting that he pulled out all the money he had in his pocket ($14.50) and said, "Here just buy it for them already."

1967 – The Le Sueur County Historical Society opened the building as a museum.

Currently – The building is still being used as a museum.

Investigation

With so many accounts of strange things happening at the museum, the stories have been divided into the areas of the museum where they take place.

MINNESOTA ROAD GUIDE TO HAUNTED LOCATIONS

The Main Entry Way. While employees were upstairs working on the museum newsletter, they heard the downstairs service bell ring. However, the employees felt that the distinct ring of the bell came from directly outside their door. When they investigated, they found that no one was downstairs and the door buzzer had not rung, which meant no one had entered the building.

While starting her workday, an employee was at the bottom of the first floor steps when she heard the giggly laugh of a young child. Curious, she walked up to the second floor to ask the director if her granddaughter was in the building. The employee was eerily surprised to find that no child was in the building.

Employees were engaged in their yearly spring clean when they witnessed a normal can of soda sitting on the counter by the service bell flip over on its side for no apparent reason.

A young girl made fun of the ghosts by sticking her tongue out into the air when someone mentioned the spirits living in the museum. Moments later, the girl entered the restroom, and as she tried to exit, she discovered that the bathroom door would not open. The girl stated that it felt as though someone or something was holding it shut from the outside. After several unsuccessful attempts to open the door, the girl gave up. After waiting several minutes, she tried to open the door again, this time it popped open without a problem.

While working at the museum, an employee heard the door to the basement creak. The woman was curious because she had never heard that door creak before. When she went to investigate, she found that the door had apparently closed on its own. It should be noted, that it takes special effort in order for someone to make the door emit any sound.

MINNESOTA ROAD GUIDE TO HAUNTED LOCATIONS

While standing in the museum lobby with two visitors, Nancy heard a loud banging noise coming from the basement where two other visitors were located. As the banging noise continued, Nancy became fearful that the couple were breaking museum pieces. She raced to the basement and asked the visitors what they were doing. Much to her surprise, they had not broken anything. The baffled couple informed Nancy that they too had heard the banging noise, but thought it was coming from the upstairs room.

The Cloakroom. An employee was working on the museum's electronic typewriter and walked away for a short moment. The employee then heard the typewriter start to type by itself. Hurrying over to the typewriter, the employee discovered six or seven random letters had been typed by some unseen force.

4 SOUTHWESTERN MINNESOTA

One day while Nancy was busy cleaning, she felt something drop on her back. At first, she thought it was a stray bat that had gotten into the museum. Yet when she checked, nothing was on her back or on the floor near her.

The 1900s Room. One of the museum's pieces is an old 1909 Edison phonograph. While Nancy was dusting in the nearby bedroom, she heard music coming from the phonograph. Knowing that the museum uses pencils to block the cylinder from turning, Nancy followed the music over to the phonograph only to find the cylinder was not turning. With the phantom music still playing, Nancy quickly left the room.

An alarm went off in the 1900's room when all the shelves mysteriously fell off the wall they were hanging on. The staff was completely puzzled, as the shelves had been on the same wall for over 35 years without ever falling off.

The Basement. Nancy was downstairs turning on all of the museum lights for the afternoon when she heard a loud crashing noise that sounded exactly like a toilet seat being slammed down. She walked over to the restroom only to discover that the toilet seat was in the upright position.

While giving a group a tour of the museum, Nancy was in the washing machine room explaining that psychics often told her that this room had a lot of paranormal activity. While she was explaining what the psychics had said, she quickly noticed that the visitors were looking over her shoulder at the door behind her. As she twirled around, she witnessed the door swaying back and forth on its own.

As you venture downstairs to the museum's basement, you will undoubtedly notice that the museum has a large old rug loom. One day while oiling the loom, a volunteer felt something gently touch the back of her neck. When she spun around no one was there.

Several employees were cleaning up in the old boiler room, when two employees bent over by the air duct and heard what sounded like many voices talking at once. Immediately thinking that some visitors had arrived at the museum, the staff hurried upstairs to find that the place was completely empty.

A three-year-old girl and her mother were cleaning the washing machine room. The young girl seemed to be talking to someone, and when she was asked whom she was speaking to, the girl replied "the little girl."

4 SOUTHWESTERN **MINNESOTA**

MINNESOTA ROAD GUIDE TO HAUNTED LOCATIONS

Janesville Doll House

Location: Janesville, Waseca County, Minnesota

Directions: Take County Road 14 (west 1st Street) to Janesville. The house will be on the north side of the street.

Ghost Lore

In the small town of Janesville is a haunted house that has become a local tourist attraction. In the attic window is a ghostly doll that keeps a vigilant watch over the townspeople. According to many, the doll itself is haunted and some even say it's alive. People claim to see the eyes move or the head turn. The doll will mysteriously change its appearance based on the seasons and the weather. In the winter it wears a little winter jacket and winter hat. If it's raining, it wears a raincoat and rain hat. If the weather's warm, the doll might even be nude. There are disagreements over whether the doll is male or female.

A variety of legends have sprung up surrounding the doll and the meaning behind it.

- Many years ago a single mother lived in the house with her 9-year-old daughter. One night, the daughter became possessed by a demon, and the young girl hanged herself from the attic window. Now the girl haunts the house, and, for reasons unknown, her mother hung a doll in the window as some kind of macabre effigy of her daughter.

- A young girl who was abused and neglected by her parents and even hated and despised by her peers and townspeople, takes her own life by hanging herself in the attic. After her death, her parents hang the doll in the window as a memorial to her.

- A shapeshifting demon lives in the attic and disguises himself as the doll. He puts curses on the people who come by to look at him.

- A man who lived here went berserk and murdered his daughter. In other versions, it's a son that's murdered.

- A young boy lives here and is being held captive in the attic by his abusive parents.
- An old man lives here, and the house is haunted by his dead wife.

Investigation

An eccentric old gentleman by the name of Ward Wendt has owned the house for many years. Nobody we talked to knows the exact year that the doll first appeared in the window, but many people recall seeing it since 1967.

Mr. Wendt, 77, is a collector who owns an old railroad car that Franklin Delano Roosevelt once rode in.

The faded porcelain doll is of a young boy about 4-5 years of age. His head is cocked slightly to his right. The doll sits in front of the window, contrary to the any reports that he hangs there. He is wearing a cloth shirt, but none of the people we spoke with ever recalled seeing any changes of wardrobe.

Local authorities advised us that there were no police reports of deaths, suicides, or abused children in the house.

Many people do insist that the house is haunted. Only Mr. Wendt knows the truth about the doll, and he's not talking. He says the full story is buried in a time capsule that will be opened in about 200 years. According to some people, the time capsule is buried in the local park. Others believe it is buried in his yard.

MINNESOTA ROAD GUIDE TO HAUNTED LOCATIONS

Sanborn Cemetery

Location: Lamberton, Redwood County, Minnesota
Address: 100th St., Lamberton, MN 56152-1194

Directions: From Highway 14 turn south on Highway 71. Continue approximately 3 miles to 100th Street. Turn west and the cemetery will be on the hill to your right.

Ghost Lore

Sanborn cemetery provides one with a glimpse of what a stereotypical haunted cemetery should look like. Perched on top of a small hill on the outskirts of a rural town, the cemetery exudes eeriness.

- A young girl was buried alive in the cemetery.
- Witnesses hear the sounds of a female crying.

4 SOUTHWESTERN MINNESOTA

- An apparition of a female has been sighted on the hill.
- At night, certain graves will glow in the cemetery.

Investigation

We found no evidence of a young girl being buried alive in the cemetery. There are several gravesites of young women in the cemetery.

Many of the townspeople heard that the ghost is that of a young kid maybe 2-4 years old.

Others confuse this cemetery with the 'glowing' cemetery. The nearby glowing cemetery is caused by a streetlight shinning on a tombstone.

We spoke with a witness that was in the cemetery one evening when she noticed a strange ball of light moving around the cemetery. This was enough to spook her into leaving.

MINNESOTA ROAD GUIDE TO HAUNTED LOCATIONS

A woman who works near the cemetery stated that she has been to the cemetery numerous times and always gets an uncomfortable feeling while there. On one trip, she heard the sounds of a young girl playing, yet was unable to locate the source.

A young man was visiting the cemetery late one night when he heard what sounded like screams coming from somewhere inside the cemetery. Although he searched the cemetery, he was unable to find the source of the ghostly screams.

4 SOUTHWESTERN **MINNESOTA**

Old Brewery Hill Spook Light

Location: Le Sueur, Le Sueur County, Minnesota

Directions: From Le Sueur, drive approximately one mile south on the Ottawa Rd. Old Brewery Hill is on the east side and the railroad tracks are on the west side.

Ghost Lore

Several years ago an old hermit was living in a cave that was part of the ruins of an old brewery south of Le Sueur. The hermit died in the cave, and his body was never found.

His ghost will emerge from the cave carrying a red lantern, and he will walk up and down the Omaha railroad tracks swinging his lantern. If you approach him, he will vanish into thin air.

MINNESOTA ROAD GUIDE TO HAUNTED LOCATIONS

History

It was probably around 1875 when George Kienzli started the brewery. He dug two cellars into the limestone hills about a mile south of Le Sueur. In one cellar he aged the beer in huge wooden barrels. The other cellar was packed with ice and used to keep the beer cold in the summer. His small business employed about three or four men, and he sold the beer to the surrounding towns of Le Sueur, Arlington, and Henderson.

George Kienzli stored kegs of beer in a cellar dug into the side of Old Brewery Hill. 1875. *Photo courtesy of The Le Sueur Museum.*

In 1895, Emil Vollbrecht purchased the Le Sueur Brewery for $3,000. He ran it for a short time, then closed it.

Peter Arbes, Sr. was the next owner. It was at this time that rumors began to circulate about the brewery being haunted. Again, the brewery went out of business and this time permanently.

All that remains of the brewery today is a limestone cave in the woods on the Tohal property east of the Ottawa road, one mile south of Le Sueur. The buildings burned down years ago.

Investigation

At one point the cave was searched and the investigation turned up some old clothes, a box, a straw mattress, and some human bones.

The Kienzli Brewery on the Ottawa Road in 1875. *Photo courtesy of The Le Sueur Museum.*

For a long time, people refused to live in the house near the brewery ruins. Most people only lived there for a short time before moving out. A Native American family, who lived there the longest, encountered tragedy when two of their sons were killed. One was killed on the railroad tracks and the other drowned. Both deaths occurred in the early fall, about the time that the ghost of the wandering hermit is said to appear.

Local people have reported hearing loud rumbling noises coming from the cave, as if there was some type of machinery running. Upon inspection, they found the cave to be empty.

On at least one occasion, a passing train saw the red lantern and was forced to stop. After an extensive search, they were unable to find the man they were certain they saw on the tracks.

Note: *The remains of the cellar are on private property, and we do not advocate trespassing. Also, the railroad tracks are extremely dangerous, and we advise people to keep clear of them.*

Montgomery Golf Course

Location: Montgomery, Le Sueur County, Minnesota
Address: 900 Rogers Dr., Montgomery, MN 56069-1328
Phone: (507) 364-5602
Website: www.MontgomeryGolfClub.com

Directions: From Hwy 26 turn north on 5th Street NE. Turn left on Hickory Ave NE. Turn right on Rodgers Dr, and arrive at the golf course.

Ghost Lore

This county golf course is surrounded by lush woods, water and some beautiful scenery. However, many guests report that more than just gophers live on this golf course.

- There are several gravesites on the course.

- The clubhouse is haunted by one of the founders of the golf course.
- A former farmer still haunts the land.
- The clubhouse TVs will turn on and off on their own.

Many believe the golf course is haunted by at least two spirits. One of the ghosts is reported to be the farmer that used to live on the current golf club grounds and is actually buried on the first hole. He will watch the clubhouse from various locations on the course as the employees lock up at night wearing a hat and overalls. The second ghost is of one of the golf club founders. He has been spotted sitting at the bar and peering in windows as, again, employees lock up at night. Televisions have turned on by themselves long after they have been turned off, and the air conditioner dial will mysteriously turn itself down past 50 degrees without anyone touching it.

History

1960s–late – Local business leaders purchased approximately 140 acres of land from Alfred Bury's wife. The land was purchased to construct a golf course.

1970 – The golf course was built on the Alfred Bury farm. It was the first golf course constructed by Minnesota golf course designer, Joel Goldstrand.

1993 – Goldstrand returned to Montgomery to design an additional nine holes and a driving range.

1994 – The golf course opened a second nine holes, giving it 18 total holes.

Investigation

There are indeed two gravestones under a large cottonwood tree on the first hole of the golf course. Unfortunately, one of the gravestones broke in a fall, yet the owners are having it repaired. The remaining gravestone lists the Buriis:

> Barbara
> Born October 6,1799, Died December 12, 1879
>
> Bendicht (Born in Switzerland)
> Born March 25, 1795, Died March 14, 1867

We spoke with several staff who had not had any personal experiences with the paranormal while working at the golf course.

4 SOUTHWESTERN MINNESOTA

We also spoke with the course manager who had heard the stories, yet did not know the origin of them.

Witnesses report seeing the ghost of a man wearing a hat and overalls. Due to his appearance, they get the impression that he is a farmer.

Other former employees report that the air conditioner in the clubhouse will act independently of the setting and also turn itself to a cold setting.

MINNESOTA ROAD GUIDE TO HAUNTED LOCATIONS

Pipestone Museum

Location: Pipestone, Pipestone County, Minnesota
Address: 113 S. Hiawatha Ave., Pipestone, MN 56164-1664
Phone: (507) 825-2563
Email: pipctymu@rconnect.com

Ghost Lore

Spirits from the past wander the museum.

History

1896 – This building was constructed and used as the old city hall for Pipestone. It was constructed of locally quarried Sioux quartzite at a cost of $8,000. This massive structure originally housed the city offices, jail, fire department, public library, and a meeting hall.

1967 – The building became the Pipestone County Historical Museum.

1976 – It was listed on the National Register of Historic Places.

Investigation

We spoke with a former employee of the museum who confirmed that the museum has had a long history of haunting activity that included cold spots, footsteps, and strange sounds.

He described an incident that occurred when the museum had a WW II exhibit that included Nazi uniforms and equipment. Employees had a problem with one particular pair of boots that seemed to keep jumping from the display shelf. It seemed that every time they left the room, they would return only to find the boots had moved from the shelf to the floor.

After researching the background information on the boots, it was later discovered that the footwear was actually from a Nazi prison camp and had belonged to a Jewish victim of the Holocaust. Apparently there was a restless spirit who didn't like his boots sitting on the shelf next to the Nazi artifacts.

TWIN CITIES MINNESOTA

Regal Cinemas

Location: Brooklyn Center, Hennepin County, Minnesota
Address: 6420 Camden Ave. N., Brooklyn Center, MN 55430-1966
Phone: (763) 566-3456

Directions: From MN 252 North turn left on 66th Avenue North. Then turn left on Camden Avenue.

Ghost Lore

People go to the movies for a variety of different reasons. Some go for a short escape from their lives, while others simply go to be entertained. Still others go to the movies to be scared. However, moviegoers usually expect to be scared by the movie, not the theatre.

- A construction worker who passed away during construction still haunts the theatre.

- Strange noises can be heard throughout the complex.
- A ghostly footprint can be seen in one of the theatres.

Investigation

The main hauntings seems to be centered around theatre number ten. It is in theatre ten, that the construction worker is said to have died. We were unable to confirm the death of a construction worker.

We spoke with two staff members who had heard of the hauntings, but had no personal experiences.

Visitors have reported hearing strange noises coming from the roof of the theatre.

There is a footprint located on the sidewall of theatre ten. It is believed to have been accidentally left by a worker when the theatre was being constructed.

While getting movies set up to play, a former worker often reported hearing footsteps upstairs when no one was present.

Schmitt Music Centers

Location: Brooklyn Center, Hennepin County, Minnesota
Address: 2400 Freeway Blvd., Brooklyn Center, MN 55430-1709
Phone: (763) 566-4560

Ghost Lore

Throughout most music centers, one can usually hear the sounds of people practicing the piano, guitar, and drums. However, many staff and customers report hearing mysterious phantom sounds that can not be so easily identified.

- A ghost continues to play various instruments after death.
- The ghost of a former piano salesman still haunts the building.
- A homeless man died right outside the backdoor and now haunts the store.

Investigation

We found that the stories of ghosts haunting the music store go back nearly 20 years.

The retail space of the store is connected with the warehouse where all the surplus instruments are kept.

We were unable to find the name of the piano salesman who passed away in the store. However, several current employees reported that the man had indeed died near the entrance of the store.

We were also unable to find the report of any homeless person dying outside the building. Yet again, current employees informed us that in 2001, the man died while trying to scratch his way inside the building. Employees also stated that the scratch marks from the man were once visible on the building's back entrance door.

Several employees report that in the evening, when they are closing up the store, they hear the sounds of someone playing an instrument. Convinced that no one is in the building, they try to locate the mysterious sounds. The staff is puzzled when they can never find a cause for the mysterious sounds.

One female employee was closing up the store when she distinctly heard someone playing the piano. After checking the entire store and finding no source of the music, the woman was extremely shaken. She was so frightened by the experience that she refused to work evenings alone.

Other employees report hearing strange noises while they close the store. The noises sound as though someone is in the building, yet when the staff investigates, no one can be found.

MINNESOTA ROAD GUIDE TO HAUNTED LOCATIONS

7 TWIN CITIES **MINNESOTA**

Maplewood Community Center

Location: Maplewood, Ramsey County, Minnesota
Address: 2100 White Bear Ave. N., Maplewood, MN 55109-3710
Phone: (651) 249- 2100

Directions: From Minnehaha Avenue East turn south onto White Bear Avenue.

Ghost Lore

Community centers provide residents with an opportunity to workout, take classes, socialize, and become more involved in their community. However, the 90,000 square foot community center in Maplewood may provide the residents an opportunity to experience a ghost.

MINNESOTA ROAD GUIDE TO HAUNTED LOCATIONS

The ghost of a young boy that drowned in the community center's pool haunts the center. The young boy is said to grab at the legs of unsuspecting swimmers. Many believe that the ghost is trying to pull other swimmers down with him.

Another version of the story states that the young boy had died on the farm and was buried near the Ramsey County Fairground land—the same land where the community center now sits.

Others believe that the center is haunted because it unwisely chose a Native American burial ground to construct the community center. The upset native spirits are blamed for much of the paranormal happenings that take place at the center.

History

Prior to the community center being built, the land was part of a farmstead and also used for some light industry.

The community center opened in October of 1994.

Investigation

We were unable to confirm that the community center land was once a Native American burial ground.

The 11-acre site does contain a swimming pool, along with a gym, theatre, and banquet center.

We spoke with several employees who had heard stories of the ghost but did not have any personal experiences. The employees reported that the stories have been around for at least five to six years.

Employees reported that several visitors reported that they felt someone tug on their legs while they were swimming in the center's pool. Others reported strange noises while in the community center.

MINNESOTA ROAD GUIDE TO HAUNTED LOCATIONS

Old Guthrie Theater

Location: Minneapolis, Hennepin County, Minnesota
Address: 725 Vineland Pl., Minneapolis, MN 55403-1139
Box Office: (612) 377-2224
Toll-free: 1-877-44STAGE
TTY: (612) 377-6626
Website: www.guthrietheater.org

Ghost Lore

While we frequently hear reports of deceased actors haunting theaters, the Guthrie Theater is unique in its stories of a ghostly usher.

- The ghost of the usher patrols his aisle in Row 18 during the performances after the lights are turned down.
- He has been seen in other locations, such as the catwalks, the elevators, tunnels, and a select section of seats known as the Queen's Box.

- A piano was heard to play on its own.
- Stage lights, props, seats, and doors have been seen to move on their own.
- Theatergoers sitting in Row 18 have had their programs yanked out of their hands and tossed into the air by an invisible entity.
- A vaporous entity was seen floating through the lounge door, then hovering in the center of the room.

History

1959 – Sir Tyrone Guthrie and his colleagues Oliver Rea and Peter Zeisler made plans for a theater.

1963 – The 1,441-seat Guthrie Theater, designed by architect Ralph Rapson, opened in Minneapolis.

1970 – A new facility opened. It shared a common entrance and lobby with the Walker Art Center.

1971 – Sir Tyrone Guthrie passed away. He was succeeded as artistic director by Michael Langham (1971-77), Alvin Epstein (1977-80), Liviu Ciulei (1980-85), Garland Wright (1986-94), Joe Dowling (1995-present).

2006 – A new, multistage Guthrie Theater was built on the banks of the Mississippi River in downtown Minneapolis. The original Guthrie Theater location was closed. *Hamlet* being their final performance.

Investigation

Richard Miller was born in Manhattan, Kansas and moved with his family to Minneapolis. While attending Edina-Morningside High School, and only 16 years old, he was hired as an usher at the Guthrie Theater. The young boy was what many today would consider to be a geek or nerd. Most kids taunted him, and he had few friends.

7 TWIN CITIES **MINNESOTA**

When he turned 18, he lived in Territorial Hall while attending the University of Minnesota. After receiving bad grades and suffering a skiing accident, the lonely, young man reached the breaking point. He quit his job, walked into a Sears store on East Lake Street, purchased a surplus Mauser rifle and some shells, and shot himself in the head while sitting in the front seat of his car. He was wearing his Guthrie Theater usher's uniform at the time of his death, and in his suicide note he requested to be buried in the same uniform. Apparently, his job at the Guthrie was the only meaningful thing in his life. Per his request, he was indeed buried in the uniform at Fort Snelling National Cemetery.

Shortly after his death, strange things began to happen at the Guthrie Theater. Theatergoers sitting in Row 18 would complain about a mysterious usher who kept pacing up and down the aisle. Their description matched that of Miller's, right down to the large mole on his cheek.

Over the years dozens of actors, ushers, custodians, and patrons have been eyewitness to the specter wearing his usher uniform.

In 1994, the visitations were so frequent that an exorcism or spiritual cleansing was performed by a Native American shaman in the hopes of calming the restless spirit and putting a stop to the haunting. Some people say the activity had halted; others claimed they could still feel the presence of the phantom usher of the Guthrie Theater.

As of this writing the fate of the Guthrie Theater is unknown. The Walker Art Center intends to tear it down, but there is a growing movement to save it. The National Trust for Historic Preservation put the theater on its list of the most endangered historic properties.

MINNESOTA ROAD GUIDE TO HAUNTED LOCATIONS

Washington Street Bridge

Location: Minneapolis, Hennepin County, Minnesota
Address: University of Minnesota, Minneapolis, MN

Directions: Follow I-35W north to the U of M east bank exit, 17C. Continue to the Washington Avenue Bridge.

Ghost Lore

Bridges are often the site of many paranormal happenings. The main function of a bridge is to provide a safe manner in which to cross over water. Yet many see this connection of the dry world and the wet world as symbolic of connecting the spirit world with the living world.

Bridges are also the site of many tragic suicides. The Washington Street Bridge is said to be haunted by the spirits of the numerous people who have taken their lives by jumping into the river. The bridge is rumored to be a hot spot for suicide activity. Among the more well-known suicides was that of a university professor.

- The ghost of a suicide victim still haunts the old bridge.
- The bridge is haunted by an escaped psychiatric patient.
- Mysterious footsteps follow students through the tunnel.

History

1884 – According to the Minnesota Historical Society, an iron truss bridge was constructed to connect Washington on both sides of the Mississippi River. The area underneath the bridge was known as the Bohemian Flats. Due to continual flooding, residents were forced to relocate, and the area was used for shipping.

1890 – The bridge was reinforced due to the rise in streetcars running between St. Paul and Minneapolis.

1954 – The rail service ended.

1965 – The original bridge was torn down.

1970s – An enclosure was added to the top of the bridge to provide shelter from the elements to those walking across. Until this time, the top of the bridge was an open space. This enclosure was intended to have heat, yet due to the costs of heating the area, the plans were scrapped.

1997 – University of Minnesota President Mark Yudof started to take pride in the university campaign. The top levels of the bridge were painted in the university's colors of maroon and gold.

2000 – The rest of the structure was stripped of its lead paint and recoated with a more aesthetic paint job.

7 TWIN CITIES **MINNESOTA**

Investigation

The historic double-decked Washington Street Bridge crosses the Mississippi River and connects the East Bank and West Bank campuses of the University of Minnesota. While the lower portion is used for vehicle traffic, the upper portion is used for pedestrians and bikes. There are specific lanes for bikes on the north side of the bridge.

We found that so many people have committed suicide from this bridge, that it is dubbed one of the most popular suicide spots in the city. One of the most noted suicides was John Berryman, a professor at the University of Minnesota. The City Pages reported that on a Friday morning in 1972, Berryman who had been sober for six months, had fallen off the wagon by drinking the better part of a bottle of whiskey the night before his death. There was also speculation that Berryman was upset over failed relationships.

A psychiatric patient did die after jumping off the bridge. However, the patient was discharged from the University Hospital and not an escapee.

Many students report that while walking over the bridge late at night, they hear ghostly footsteps following them. When the students stop to look around, no one is found. When the students continue, so do the ghostly footsteps.

7 TWIN CITIES **MINNESOTA**

Fitzgerald Theatre

Location: Saint Paul, Ramsey County, Minnesota
Address: 10 Exchange St. E., St. Paul, MN 55101-2220
Phone: (651) 290-1221

Directions: Follow 10th Street to Cedar Street and turn right. Go one block to Exchange Street and turn right. The Fitzgerald is located on Exchange between Cedar and Wabasha Streets.

Ghost Lore

The Fitzgerald Theatre is best known as the theatre where the immensely popular radio show A Prairie Home Companion was taped. Yet, the theatre had a rich and colorful history of its own long before Garrison Keillor, including being the home for a great deal of ghostly activity.

- Haunted by a former stagehand who is frequently seen around the theatre.
- Those who work in the theatre repeatedly hear their names being called by something unseen.
- The ghost of an unknown woman roams the historic theatre.
- Unexplained cold spots can be felt in the theatre.

History

1910 – The Sam S. Shubert theatre was constructed as one of four memorial theatres by Lee and J.J. Shubert for their brother Sam. The theatre was constructed after the famous Maxine Elliot Theatre in New York. With a movable stage, 16 dressing rooms, and almost

2,000 stage lights, the theatre was touted as one of the finest theatres of the time.

1933 – The theatre was used to screen foreign films. The theatre was thus dubbed the World Theatre.

Throughout the years, the theatre became run down and dilapidated.

1980 – The theatre was purchased by Minnesota Public Radio.

1985 – After much renovation, the theatre was once again opened to the public.

1994 – The theatre was renamed after Minnesota author F. Scott Fitzgerald.

Currently the theatre is used for plays, concerts, and musicals.

MINNESOTA ROAD GUIDE TO HAUNTED LOCATIONS

Investigation

One of the main ghosts is believed to be a former worker named Ben. Ben is thought to have worked in the theatre during the early 1900's. According to the staff, Ben is most often seen up in the catwalk of the theatre.

We spoke with an employee who was working at the front desk, when he stepped out of the room for a moment. Upon his return, he noticed that his desk chair had inexplicably moved into the lobby. The man was extremely puzzled, as the only way to get the chair into the lobby would have been through him.

While working, a female employee saw the ghostly apparition of a man walking about the theatre. She was so scared by her sighting that she immediately called her husband to come pick her up while she waited outside the theatre.

Several staff members have reported seeing a strange shadowy figure pass by them while they are working in the theatre.

7 TWIN CITIES MINNESOTA

MINNESOTA ROAD GUIDE TO HAUNTED LOCATIONS

While completing renovations on the historic theatre, construction workers would show up to work to find that their tools were moved around or even missing. Old antiques would mysteriously be discovered in the theatre.

The female ghost of the theatre is thought to be a former actress named Veronica. The sounds of a female voice singing are often attributed to her.

7 TWIN CITIES **MINNESOTA**

Forepaugh's Restaurant

Location: Saint Paul, Ramsey County, Minnesota
Address: 276 Exchange St. S., St. Paul MN 55102-2417
Phone: (612) 224-5606

Ghost Lore

This Victorian mansion is a centerpiece of the historic Irving Park area. Once considered by many in St. Paul as one the most exclusive residential areas in Minnesota, the area was ripe with wealth and gossip alike. With a story shrouded in suicide, adultery, depression, and mystery, all Forepaugh's needed was a ghost. And that is exactly what they got.

- Joseph Forepaugh was having an affair with a housemaid named Molly. When his wife found out, she forbid him from seeing Molly. It was his wife's decision of ending his affair that is said to have caused Forepaugh's downward spiral of depression.

MINNESOTA ROAD GUIDE TO HAUNTED LOCATIONS

- Many in the community believed Forepaugh killed himself over financial matters, while others believed he was heartbroken over having to end his affair with Molly.

- The ghost of the housemaid that killed herself on the third floor still haunts the restaurant. Many believe that she was also pregnant with Forepaugh's child.

- Forepaugh himself still wanders his old home searching for his lost love.

History

1870 – Joseph Forepaugh constructed a majestic home for his wife Mary. It was constructed at the cost of $10,000. Joseph was part owner in a huge wholesaler of dry goods and was considered a master businessman at the young age of 36.

1872 – A carriage house was built on the grounds.

1879 – A large addition to the home was constructed.

1886 – The house was sold to General John Henry Hammond, a general from the civil war.

1886-1889 – The Forepaughs spent time traveling around Europe. It was during this time that Joseph suffered from severe bouts of depression.

1889 – The Forepaugh family moved to St. Paul.

1892 – Joseph took his own life.

1900s – The home, and the area, fall into disrepair. Eventually the home was closed down by the Housing and Redevelopment Authority.

1974 – Forepaugh's home and its adjoining three lots were purchased by Naegele Restaurant No Limit, Inc. The home was gutted and completely renovated.

1983 – The home was again sold as a restaurant.

Currently – The building is used as Forepaugh's Restaurant.

Investigation

Mr. Forepaugh did commit suicide. His dead body was discovered in 1892. He shot himself in the head with a revolver that was found clenched in his hand. Immediately people thought he had killed himself over bad finances. However, it was soon uncovered that at the time of his death, Forepaugh had an estimated wealth of over $500,000.

We also found that a housemaid named Molly did hang herself on the third floor of the home. We found no evidence that she was pregnant with Forepuagh's child. Staff believe that Molly hanged herself where the chandelier is now located.

We spoke with an employee that was working one evening and had just finished straightening the closet's hangers, and when she turned around, all the hangers were moved to one side.

Several employees reported seeing the ghost of an arrogant looking man walking around the dining area. The employees state that the ghost acts as though he owns the place.

Many customers and staff report seeing the ghost of a woman dressed in Victorian garb roaming through the dining area. When staff and customers go to investigate, the woman disappears.

We spoke with several employees that reported seeing lights turn on and off on their own while they were working.

Several employees told of times while they were working in the restaurant when they seemed to have stepped into an unexplained cold spot.

One employee told us that she and other staff routinely find that the dining chairs have been flipped over for no apparent reason.

MINNESOTA ROAD GUIDE TO HAUNTED LOCATIONS

Gibbs Museum

Location: Saint Paul, Ramsey County, Minnesota
Address: 2097 Larpenteur Ave W., St. Paul, MN 55113-5313
Phone: (651) 646-8629
The Museum is closed from mid-November to mid-April

Directions: From I-94 West take exit 280. Take the Larpenteur Avenue exit and turn right on Larpenteur Avenue.

Ghost Lore

Whether it is the old furniture, the musty smell, the lack of modern conveniences, or just the unwelcoming feel, many people find old farmhouses extremely creepy. However, those who find the old Gibbs farmhouse creepy may be picking up the ghost of the property.

- The ghost of a young boy that was killed on the land still haunts the home.

- Mysterious imprints are found on the beds, as though someone has slept on them.
- Ghosts of young children have been spotted roaming around on this old farm site.
- Furniture has been seen moving on its own.

History

1833 – Five-year-old Jane DeBow was kidnapped by several missionaries traveling to Minnesota. Jane grew up in Minnesota.

1849 – Jane met and married Mr. Herman Gibbs. The newlyweds purchased land in Minnesota and relocated. Jane and Herman lived in a sod house on the land.

1854 – The Gibbs family built a small cabin, which is now one of the rooms of the farmhouse.

1867 – The bedrooms and the parlor of the farmhouse were constructed.

MINNESOTA ROAD GUIDE TO HAUNTED LOCATIONS

1874 – A kitchen was added onto the home, bringing the home to its current size.

1900 – The Gibbs family ran a garden on their property selling food to the growing town nearby.

1910 – The Gibbs family constructed the white barn on their property.

Currently – The farm is a museum operated by the Ramsey County Historical Society.

Investigation

The Gibbs' nine-year-old son William (Willy) fell ill while helping to put out a prairie fire that threatened the farmhouse. Although the family eventually succeeded in saving the farm, several days later, Willy died due to smoke inhalation.

All of the paranormal events seem to take place only in the old farmhouse and not the surrounding buildings.

A female employee was cleaning the kitchen by herself when she heard the sound of footsteps walk through the hallway directly behind her. The footsteps then proceeded to move towards the upstairs. The curious woman quickly ran up the stairs to see who was in the home. Needless to say, the woman was amazed to find that no one was upstairs.

Many of the tour guides get a tense feeling while giving tours of the farmhouse. Even those who do not believe in hauntings, do not enjoy being in the building by themselves.

One of the many antiques in the home is an old rocking chair. Many staff and visitors have seen the rocking chair start rocking on its own, when no was in it.

Many of the staff have reported seeing the doors and cupboards of the old farmhouse opening and closing on their own.

Former staff members recall that the toys from the toy room would be locked in the chest for the evening. When the workers would come back the next morning, they would find that the toys were mysteriously out of the chest as though someone had been playing with them.

One of the tour guides is able to sense spirits and on one tour reported sensing a ghost of a teenage boy inside the farmhouse.

At around midnight, a sheriff's deputy was checking on the museum when he saw what appeared to be a child's face in the second story window of the main farmhouse. However, staff informed him that it could not have been a boy that he saw because the building was empty during the time of his sighting.

One of the skeptical tour guides was leisurely sitting on the farmhouse's front porch bench when she looked into a window and noticed that there was a young kid in the house. The woman was

7 TWIN CITIES MINNESOTA

extremely surprised, as she knew no one was in the home at the time.

The former manager, who was known to be a prankster, reported that each day when he opened, he would find an indentation on one of the beds as though someone had slept on it. None of the staff that we talked with had ever seen an indentation on any of the beds.

Landmark Center

Location: Saint Paul, Ramsey County, Minnesota
Address: 75 5th St. W., St. Paul, MN 55102-1431
Phone: (612) 292-3233

Ghost Lore

In St. Paul, having a building that is connected to gangsters is relatively common, however most of the buildings the gangsters frequented were not set up to prosecute them. This is where the Landmark Center differs, as stories of a former gangster that still haunts the site of his conviction still flourish.

- Bottles of booze mysteriously tip over or are inexplainably misplaced.

- Elevator doors open and close on their own.

7 TWIN CITIES **MINNESOTA**

- Wedding guests often report seeing uninvited guests throughout the building.
- A ghost continues to haunt the restrooms of the historic building.

History

The building was constructed in 1902 to serve as the federal courthouse and post office for the people of the Midwest.

1902-1960s – The Ramsey County Room served as the courtroom of some of the country's most infamous gangsters including Baby Face Nelson, John Dillinger, Ma Barker, and Machine Gun Kelly. This room was also the site where Jack Peifer was convicted.

1936 – Gangster Jack Peifer was tried and convicted on charges of kidnapping. Jack later committed suicide in his jail cell.

1970s – Concerned citizens fueled on restoring the historic building were able to save the building from certain destruction. This same group began the arduous process of trying to bring the building back to the glory days of its youth.

1978 – The Landmark Center was designated as a National Historic Monument and was re-opened to the general public.

Investigation

Many of the staff believe that the building is haunted by gangster Jack Peifer. Doug Mack, in his article, "In Search of Jack, Gangster and Ghost," writes that Jack was a bellhop and worked his way up the gangster ladder, and eventually became a banker for

7 TWIN CITIES MINNESOTA

mobsters. Mack also found that Jack owned a speakeasy that was frequented by many of St. Paul's gangsters during the 1920s and 30s. Jack then hooked up with the nefarious Karpis-Barkergand gang, and was a main culprit in the kidnapping of a well-known brewery heir. Jack was convicted of his crimes on the third floor of the Landmark building.

We spoke with a security guard who reported that on many nights while he was making his rounds he would approach the elevators on the third floor, only to have them open for him. This was the floor that Jack was tried and convicted on, and the guard believed that Jack, being a former bellhop, was still doing his job.

One evening while attending a wedding, a female guest was washing up in the restroom when she heard the sound of a strange man laughing behind her. When she spun around to see the laughing man, no one was there.

Visitors and staff in the building report seeing the stall doors in the women's bathroom open and close on their own.

MINNESOTA ROAD GUIDE TO HAUNTED LOCATIONS

Many staff and guests report seeing bottles of gin and whisky fall over on their own, and shot glasses are often broken for no apparent reason.

At the information desk, the staff keep a photo from a previous wedding that purportedly shows the face of a ghost lurking behind a young ring bearer. The photo was sent to the Landmark Center after a wedding couple discovered it on their film.

7 TWIN CITIES **MINNESOTA**

Minnesota State Fair

Location: Saint Paul, Ramsey County, Minnesota
Physical Address: State Fair Grounds, Saint Paul, MN
Mailing Address: 1265 Snelling Ave. N., St. Paul, MN 55108-3003
Phone: (651) 288-4400
TTY: (651) 642-2372
Website: www.mnstatefair.org

Ghost Lore

Although many people find the notion of standing in line to buy a deep fried candy bar scary, the Minnesota State Fair boosts something even scarier, a history of ghosts.

- A mysterious reincarnated bird is said to appear at the same ride each year.

- Visitors report a phantom animal in one of the fair's barns.
- Several ghosts have been spotted enjoying all the various themes to the fair.

History

1855-1858 – The fair was held at several points throughout Minnesota.

1859 – The Minnesota State Fair was held near what has become downtown Minneapolis.

1861 & 1862 – The fair was not held due to the Civil War.

1884 – A committee was selected by the Minnesota State Agricultural Society with the task of selecting a permanent site for the fair. The new site was chosen because it was nearly halfway between St. Paul and Minneapolis.

7 TWIN CITIES **MINNESOTA**

1885 – The fair was held in its new location. This is the spot where the fair is currently located.

1893 – The fair was not held due to a scheduling conflict with the World's Columbian Exposition in Chicago.

1901 – Vice President Theodore Roosevelt first uttered his famous line of "Speak softly and carry a big stick" in a speech delivered at the Minnesota State Fair.

1945 – The fair was not held due to WW II fuel shortages.

1946 – The fair was not held due to a polio epidemic.

Currently – The fair attracts over one and a half million visitors each year.

Investigation

The bird said to visit the historic Ye Old Mill ride is believed to be the reincarnated spirit of a former fair worker named Wayne

Murray. We spoke with several employees of the ride who had never heard of the bird. The Ye Old Mill is one of the oldest rides at the state fair.

We were unable to find any witnesses that had spotted the phantom pig that was once said to haunt the swine barn of the fair.

We spoke with several employees who had heard of the State Fair ghosts, yet had never had a personal experience.

Both the *St. Paul Pioneer Press* and the *Minneapolis Star Tribune* have published stories of fair visitors who have seen ghosts that are walking around the fair among the other visitors. According to the papers, the ghosts have been spotted near the grandstand, and walking within the crowds.

7 TWIN CITIES **MINNESOTA**

Wabasha Street Caves

Location: Saint Paul, Ramsey County, Minnesota
Address: 215 Wabasha St. S., St. Paul, MN 55107-1805
Phone: (651) 224-1191
Website: www.wabashastreetcaves.com

Directions: Take South Wabasha Street to the Caves.

Ghost Lore

Gangsters, murder, fine dining, disco dancing, and glass are all small parts of the Wabasha Street Cave's sorted past. A favorite hang out spot for some of St. Paul's most notorious gangsters, the caves still hold several unexplained mysteries.

- The ghosts of gangsters killed in the caves still haunt their old speakeasy.

MINNESOTA ROAD GUIDE TO HAUNTED LOCATIONS

- Many report strange balls of lights roaming through the caves.
- Many visitors report hearing the sounds of a phantom band playing in the caves.

History

The caves started out as a mushroom farm and during the early 1900s the caves were the largest producer of mushrooms in the United States. The caves were also plentiful with silica, and much of it was sold to make glass for the booming expansion of the automobile.

1900s – The caves were used as a speakeasy called the Wabasha Street Speakeasy and cave seven was used as a whisky still.

1933 – The caves were used as a restaurant called the Castle Royal.

7 TWIN CITIES **MINNESOTA**

MINNESOTA ROAD GUIDE TO HAUNTED LOCATIONS

1930s – A table of four men were playing cards. One of the men had a large music case with him. An argument broke out, and the woman working heard machine gun fire, when she came back to see what had happened, she found three dead bodies on the floor. Immediately the police were called and they told her not to worry. When she came back to see if the police were finished, the bodies were gone and the police had cleaned up the area and told her that nothing had happened, as she must have imagined all of it.

1934 – Three young women were at the club when a gentleman approached one of them and asked her to dance. She was enthralled with the man's confidence and quickly agreed. When the man left, a fellow patron came up to the woman and asked her if she knew who she had just danced with. When she told the man she had no idea who her dance partner was, the man said, "That was John Dillinger."

1941 – The restaurant closed due to World War II. The caves reverted back to producing mushrooms.

1970s – Castle Royal 2 opened as a disco.

Currently – The caves are used as a dance hall and wedding facility along with guided tours.

Investigation

Back in the 1970's when the caves were the Castle Royal, the disco was closed when the manager and an employee saw a ghost of a man walk toward them. The man continued to walk past them and through the wall. The men stated that the "man" they saw was dressed like a gangster from the 1920s.

The current owners were in the caves with their son cleaning. The son was bouncing a tennis ball when the ball got loose and rolled into the men's bathroom. The boy reached down to pick up the ball and when he came up, he saw a ghost of a gangster in the mirror. When the boy spun around no one was there.

7 TWIN CITIES MINNESOTA

An actor went into the men's bathroom when he thought he heard music playing. The man was convinced that a big band had started playing. The man was completely baffled when he returned from the restroom to find that no band was playing.

During one of the many weddings to take place in the caves, a young boy reported that he really enjoyed playing with all of the gangsters that were at the wedding. The wedding party believed that the child had a good imagination so they ignored the young boy. However, when the wedding photos were developed, the couple discovered a strange mist in the photo with the young boy.

- Many other staff and customers report hearing the sound of music playing while in the restrooms. No source of the music can be found.

- Seven actors were rehearsing for an upcoming play with the director when they noticed a ghost of a man sitting at the table reserved for the audience.

- Actors also report a bus boy leaning on the side of a table. The bus boy always seems to just disappear into thin air.

- Bullet holes can still be seen from the card game shoot out in the Fireside room.

- The ghost of a woman has been spotted by many staff and customers roaming through the caves.

- Many employees report seeing strange globes of light floating throughout the bar area of the caves.

7 TWIN CITIES MINNESOTA

Lakeshore Players Theatre

Location: White Bear Lake, Ramsey County, Minnesota
Address: 4820 Stewart Ave., White Bear Lake, MN 55110-2837
Box Office: (651) 429-5674
Business Office: (651) 426-3275
Email: tickets@lakeshoreplayers.com
office@lakeshoreplayers.com
Website: www.lakeshoreplayers.com

Directions: From Highway 61 turn east on 7th street. Turn south on Stewart Street.

Ghost Lore

Throughout this book, you have seen haunted theatres and haunted churches. Yet the Lakeshore Player's Theatre building has combined a former church with a new theatre and even added a ghost.

MINNESOTA ROAD GUIDE TO HAUNTED LOCATIONS

- This former church is haunted by several ghosts.
- The spirit pays special attention to the females in the theatre.
- Props and costumes are mysteriously moved around the theatre.
- The ghost of a former actress has been heard throughout the theatre.

History

1890 – The building was constructed to be used as a church.

The community theatre is in its 53rd season and is the second longest running community theatre in Minnesota.

7 TWIN CITIES **MINNESOTA**

When a fire forced the group out of their old building, they moved into the church. The group then began some major renovations.

Investigation

Many of the performers have dubbed the ghost "George." The name does not seem to be based on any particular person. George is also believed to be very protective of females in the theatre.

We spoke with an employee that stated that a lot of the paranormal activity happens during times of heavy renovation of the theatre.

While working in the theatre, an employee saw the ghost of a strange man wearing an old work uniform walk right through a solid wall.

WESTERN MINNESOTA

MINNESOTA ROAD GUIDE TO HAUNTED LOCATIONS

Chanhassen Dinner Theatres

Location: Chanhassen, Carver County, Minnesota
Address: 501 W. 78th St., Chanhassen, MN 55317-9677
Box Office: (952) 934-1525
Toll-free: 1-800-362-3515
Website: www.chanhassentheatres.com

Directions: Follow State Hwy 5. Turn south on Great Plains Blvd. Take the first left past the railroad tracks into Chanhassen Dinner Theatre's parking lot.

Ghost Lore

Many people are deeply attached to their land. Often times, even after death, some people do not seem to want to leave. Theatres are often believed to be haunted for several reasons. First, many believe that all of the energy that is housed in theatres is replayed as though it is a recording. Another theory is that those involved with theatre work do it because they love it, and it only makes sense that that would stay around after their death. However, skeptics claim that witnesses are only imagining things or seeing nothing more than real people in costumes or stage props. The debate on theatres being haunted is still brewing at the Chanhassen Dinner Theatre.

- A woman named Mary, who died in an old farmhouse that burned down, still haunts the area.

- A woman that was killed on her bike while riding home from a play has come back to haunt the theatre.

- Several ghosts of those who have died while in the theatre have come back to haunt the theatre.

History

1965 – The theatre was constructed by Herb and Carol Bloomberg. At the time, the land was considered rural and was actually built on an old cornfield.

1968 – The theatre opened for audiences with its first play, *How to Succeed in Business Without Trying.*

1973 – The Bloomberg's expanded the theatre from its original size.

1978 – A bar on the property called the Bronco Bar was demolished to make room for the ever-expanding theatre.

1989 – The theatre was purchased by Tom Scallen and International Theatres Corporation.

Investigation

We found that a woman named Mary did live on the land. However, she did not die in a fire, as she died as an old woman.

We found that an actress named Marjorie was killed while riding her bike. However, she was killed many years after she was part of her one and only play at the theatre.

8 WESTERN **MINNESOTA**

MINNESOTA ROAD GUIDE TO HAUNTED LOCATIONS

Most of the ghost stories seem to have started in 1984, when several performers of the play *Quilters* reported feeling that a presence was on stage with them while they performed. This anomaly was reported several times by numerous different people. All of the witnesses reported that the spirit on stage was friendly.

Because so many performers had felt the presence of someone on stage with them, the theatre brought in a female medium to investigate the ghost stories. However, the medium was not able to make contact with any specific spirits.

Several elderly actors have passed away while performing in plays at the theatre. However, the last death in the theatre occurred nearly 20 years ago.

Many visitors of the theatre have seen a ghost of a woman peering down at them from the second floor windows.

8 WESTERN **MINNESOTA**

MINNESOTA ROAD GUIDE TO HAUNTED LOCATIONS

Visitors reported seeing the ghost of a young woman wandering throughout the Inglenook room. Many stated that she appeared to be wearing Victorian era clothing. The Inglenook room is located directly below the window where the ghost of a woman has been seen.

We spoke with the public relations officer who has been at the theatre for nearly 30 years. She informed us that she never has had a paranormal experience in the theatre, and believes the ghost stories began because of a misidentification. She reported that a former employee saw another employee emerge from behind some equipment and thought she had seen a ghost.

We also spoke with several long time employees that never had a paranormal experience at the theatre. Yet many of these employees keep an open mind while working at the theatre.

8 WESTERN MINNESOTA

Soap Box Laundromat

Location: Kimball, Stearns County, Minnesota
Address: 80 S. Main St., Kimball, MN 55353-5303
Phone: (320) 398-7627

Ghost Lore

Many of us find the task of washing clothes at a laundromat inconvenient and time-consuming. However, you may not mind washing your clothes at the Soap Box Laundromat, that is, if you can handle the ghost.

During the evenings, while washing their clothes, customers report hearing a strange crying noise coming from inside the small laundromat.

Customers report seeing the ghost of a young girl running from the door. The young girl then disappears right into a wall.

MINNESOTA ROAD GUIDE TO HAUNTED LOCATIONS

Investigation

We were unable to find a reason for the building to be haunted by a young girl.

Many of the residents of Kimball were unaware of the reported ghost at the laundromat.

This case is still pending, as we are still searching for more witnesses. We are also speaking to neighbors of the laundromat to determine if they too, have seen the ghost of the young girl.

8 WESTERN MINNESOTA

MINNESOTA ROAD GUIDE TO HAUNTED LOCATIONS

Swensson Farm Museum

Location: Montevideo, Chippewa County, Minnesota
Official Name: Olof Swensson Farm Museum
Phone: (320) 269-7636
Hours: Open Sunday afternoons Memorial Day to Labor Day 1 pm to 5 pm or by appointment.

Directions: Six miles east of Montevideo. From Highway 7 turn south on County Road 6. Turn left on County Road 15 and the farm will be on your left hand side.

Ghost Lore

Far too many of Minnesota's historic sites have been lost. Luckily for you, the Swensson family farm, burial plot, and barn still remain, for both the living and the dead to enjoy.

- Many witnesses believe that the home is haunted by one of the Swensson family members.

8 WESTERN **MINNESOTA**

- There is a long dark tunnel that runs from the graveyard to the house. Olof is said to have built the tunnel so he could hear if one of his children was accidentally buried alive.

- The cemetery housed a large bell with a long rope tied to it that the children could ring if they were buried alive.

- A large cross was discovered on the basement wall. It is said that the cross was painted in blood.

- Strange lights have been seen in the empty house by those driving by the farm during the evening.

- Olof Swensson worshiped rocks and had many other strange ideas.

History

1843 – Olof Swensson was born in Norway.

1869 – Olof married Ingleborg Agnette Pearson.

MINNESOTA ROAD GUIDE TO HAUNTED LOCATIONS

1871 – The Swenssons came to Wegdahl, Minnesota.

1878 – Their first child, Sven, died at the age of seven.

1880s – Olof and his daughter Katie constructed the foundation of the barn. This barn is the only barn in Minnesota listed on the National Registrar of Historic Places.

1901 – Swensson began work on the 22-room house.

1903 – The family home was completed by Olof and his daughter Katie at a cost of $5,000.

1923 – Olof passed away. The farm steadily declined and became dilapidated. The surviving children continued to live on the farm.

1967 – Olof's daughter Emma passed away. Two days later, her brother John, the last surviving Swensson, passed away, and the land was bequeathed to the Chippewa County Historical Society.

Investigation

Many of the Swenssons were diabetic, and often diabetics of that time would fall into a coma caused by an imbalance of sugar levels in the blood. Many of the young Swensson children did pass away. Many families feared that they would accidentally bury a loved one who was in a coma, only to have them awake to be buried alive.

We found that there is no tunnel leading from the graveyard to the house. However, there is still much debate about a warning bell being in the cemetery to alarm the family if someone was buried alive. The cemetery bell story seems more plausible as it is approximately 150 yards from the home to the graveyard. It would have been very difficult to have constructed a tunnel of that length. On the other hand, cemetery bells were not that uncommon during the years of Mr. Swensson.

We found no evidence that Olof ever worshiped rocks. However, those who knew him believed that he had many strange ideas and was a very peculiar person. The Chippewa County Historical Society did find that Olof ran for Governor of MN, had a church in his barn, and wanted to create an amendment to the Constitution of the United States. Swennson also built a mill on his land and wanted to put his competitor out of business. His competitor's name was Pillsbury.

There are nine people buried in the family cemetery, both parents and seven of the children. The other two daughters who married were not buried on the land. It is said that Olof did not want any of his daughters to marry and disowned two daughters that did marry. Therefore, those two daughters are not buried on the family plot.

We spoke with an employee who stated that many people who pass by the old farmstead report that the lights inside the home flicker on and off even though no one is in the home.

A woman driving by the farm at 4am reported seeing the house lights turn on and off on their own.

About the Authors

Chad Lewis is a paranormal investigator for Unexplained Research LLC, with a Master's Degree in Applied Psychology from the University of Wisconsin-Stout. He has spent years traveling the globe researching ghosts, strange creatures, crop formations, werewolves, and UFOs. Chad is a former State Director for the Mutual UFO Network and has worked with BLT Crop Circle Investigations. He is the organizer of the Unexplained Conferences and the host of *The Unexplained* paranormal radio talk show.

Terry Fisk is also a paranormal investigator for Unexplained Research LLC and an authority on death and the afterlife. He is a shamanic Buddhist practitioner and member of the Foundation for Shamanic Studies who studied philosophy and religion at the University of Wisconsin. Terry is the co-host of *The Unexplained* paranormal radio talk show and director for *The Unexplained* television series.

The UNEXPLAINED Presents

Wisconsin
Road Guide to
Haunted Locations
by Chad Lewis & Terry Fisk
Foreword by
Richard D. Hendricks

ISBN-13: 978-0-9762099-1-1

South Dakota
Road Guide to
Haunted Locations
by Chad Lewis & Terry Fisk
Foreword by
Michael Thomas Coffield

ISBN-13: 978-0-9762099-3-5

Credit Card Purchases Online at
www.unexplainedresearch.com

UNEXPLAINED RESEARCH
PO BOX 2173
EAU CLAIRE WI 54702-2173

The UNEXPLAINED Presents

Iowa
Road Guide to
Haunted Locations
by Chad Lewis & Terry Fisk
Foreword by
Michael Whye

ISBN-13: 978-0-9762099-4-2

Illinois
Road Guide to
Haunted Locations
by Chad Lewis & Terry Fisk
Foreword by
Scott Maruna

ISBN-13: 978-0-9762099-5-9

Credit Card Purchases Online at
www.unexplainedresearch.com

UNEXPLAINED RESEARCH
PO BOX 2173
EAU CLAIRE WI 54702-2173

The UNEXPLAINED Presents

UFO Wisconsin: A Progress Report
by Noah Voss

The definitive guide to UFO reports and investigations throughout the Dairy State.

ISBN-13: 978-0-9762099-7-3

The 13th Planet: Coming out of Darkness
by Michael Thomas Coffield

A science fiction drama full of suspense, faith, and the twist and turns that will keep you turning the pages for more.

ISBN-13: 978-0-9762099-0-4

Credit Card Purchases Online at
www.unexplainedresearch.com

HIDDEN HEADLINES

Strange, Unusual, & Bizarre Newspaper Stories 1860-1910

HIDDEN HEADLINES OF WISCONSIN
by Chad Lewis
Foreword by Michael Bie

ISBN-13: 978-0-9762099-6-6

HIDDEN HEADLINES OF TEXAS
by Chad Lewis
Foreword by Nick Redfern

ISBN-13: 978-0-9762099-8-0

HIDDEN HEADLINES OF NEW YORK
by Chad Lewis

ISBN-13: 978-0-9762099-9-7

HIDDEN HEADLINES OF CALIFORNIA
by Chad Lewis

ISBN-13: 978-0-9798822-0-3